COME THE MILLENNIUM
Interviews on the Shape of Our Future

American Society of Newspaper Editors

Introduction by Ellen Goodman

Andrews and McMeel
A Universal Press Syndicate Company
Kansas City

Come the Millennium copyright © 1994 by the American Society of Newspaper Editors. All rights reserved. Printed in the United States of America. No part of this book may be used or reproduced in any manner whatsoever without written permission except in the case of reprints in the context of reviews. For information, write Andrews and McMeel, a Universal Press Syndicate Company, 4900 Main Street, Kansas City, Missouri 64112.

Library of Congress Cataloging-in-Publication Data

Come the millenium : interviews on the shape of our future / American Society of Newspaper Editors : introduction by Ellen Goodman.
   p. cm.
   ISBN 0-8362-8070-9 : $8.95
   1. Twenty-first century—Forecasts. 2. United States—Forecasting. I. American Society of Newspaper Editors.
CB161.C643   1994
973'.0112—dc20   94-7027
                                                                       CIP

Attention: Schools and Businesses

Andrews and McMeel books are available at quantity discounts for bulk purchase for educational, business, or sales promotional use. For information, please write to Special Sales Department, Andrews and McMeel, 4900 Main Street, Kansas City, Missouri 64112.

CONTENTS

Introduction   1

MARVIN SIRBU   *Save Time and Stamps*   3
With Madelyn Ross, *Pittsburgh Post-Gazette*

HELEN VENDLER   *For Art's Sake, Folks!*   7
With Jack Driscoll, *The Boston Globe*

WILMA MANKILLER   *Tahlequah Revisited*   12
With Ed Kelley, *The Daily Oklahoman*

LINDA CHAPIN   *Farewell to Workaholism*   16
With Jane Healy, *Orlando Sentinel*

DONALD E. WORSTER   *Reinventing the West*   20
With Prof. John C. Ginn, University of Kansas

RON CROUCH   *A Scam on Ourselves*   23
With Timothy M. Kelly, *Lexington* (Kentucky) *Herald-Leader*

CRAIG J. THOMPSON   *The Techno Backlash*   27
With Frank Denton, *Wisconsin State Journal*

AMR ISMAIL   *A Recipe for Yecch*   33
With Lou Ureneck, The Portland, Maine, Newspapers

ROBERT H. THIBADEAU   *Take Me to "Heaven"*   36
With Madelyn Ross, *Pittsburgh Post-Gazette*

STEWART BRAND   *The Millennial Generation*   39
With William German and Matthew Wilson, *San Francisco Chronicle*

Contents

MICHAEL HOOKER *A Library on My Belt* **45**
With Larry McDermott, *Springfield* (Massachusetts) *Union-News* and *Sunday Republican*

ARTHUR W. ORR *Make That "Taxamerica"* **51**
With Tom Wright, *Decatur* (Alabama) *Daily*

GAYL NESS *The Unthinkable Africa* **56**
With James Tobin, *The Detroit News*

SHERRY H. PENNEY *Parlez-Vous Español?* **61**
With William B. Ketter, *The Patriot Ledger,* Quincy, Mass.

LOWELL CATLETT *A Diploma in Degrees* **68**
With Tim Gallagher, *Albuquerque Tribune*

MICHELE DEASY *Feminization of Dux* **73**
With Judy Brown, *The Herald,* New Britain, Conn.

JAGDISH SHETH *Managing Oxymorons* **76**
With Ron Martin, *Atlanta Journal and Constitution*

WINSLOW WEDIN *Invest in Coffee Shops* **88**
With John Christie, *Fort Lauderdale Sun-Sentinel*

PATRICIA B. CRONIN *Mr. and Mrs. Village* **92**
With Dan Warner, *The Lawrence* (Massachusetts) *Eagle-Tribune*

TIMOTHY J. COOLEY *Hold on to Your Socks* **98**
With Neil Wertheimer, *Orange County Register*

DAVID HAYES-BAUTISTA *Unload the Baggage* **103**
With Karen Wada, *Los Angeles Times*

Introduction

By Ellen Goodman

Like most journalists, I'm occasionally asked to make a prediction. My stock answer is that I don't "do" the future. Journalists don't do windows, we don't do predictions. Newspapers are the first draft of history, not the first guess of futurism. They are, literally, the repositories of yesterday's news, not tomorrow's.

I'm not sure why we are future-aversive. Maybe it's our work. After all, you can't report what hasn't happened. Or maybe it's our professional daily-ness. We are trained to live in "the here" and write in "the now." Our horizons are the next edition, and our sight is focused, intensely but narrowly, on deadlines.

But, after thirty years spent in newsrooms, I also think that as institutions, newspapers are peculiarly uncomfortable with change. We spend our lives reporting on change—changing governments, mores, events, technologies, societies. But we don't embrace change ourselves. We were not the first profession to diversify our staffs or to get our technology on line or to alter the size and look of our "product." And even when we think about tomorrow, or tomorrow's edition, we may not look ten or twenty years ahead.

The American Society of Newspaper Editors broke with this past when it embarked on a project to think about the decades after tomorrow. In true journalistic style, members went out to talk to doctors, lawyers, architects, poets, demographers, psychologists, educators, and citizens. If these contributors—these people who do futures—agree on anything, it's on the concept of "permanent change." And if, in turn, that sounds like an oxymoron, so be it. After all, my favorite quote comes from the interviewee who said, "the future is about managing oxymorons."

There are people in these pages who face the millennium deeply pessimistic about pollution or violence or even the demise of the arts, because "nobody sings anymore." There are others who carry a nineteenth-century optimism about progress—especially in electronic technology—into the twenty-first century. Some speak of grim reality and others of "virtual reality."

A planner from Florida says that urban life is done for and that cities are going to have to be evacuated. An educator from Massachusetts says that more Americans will be living in cities that must be restored. There are predictions about a new world that will be built along the edges of the new hi-tech information superhighway. And there are predictions that the next big growth area is in hands-on, down-home "experiences" that come from a longing for a simpler life. One of our "futurists" says that the biggest change will be the aging of America. Another reminds us that the problem of any future is, inevitably, in the hands of the families that raise the next generation. And everyone has an opinion about the place or the absence of newspapers in their future.

These conversations about the next century are the stuff of intriguing conjecture. We leave it to the next generation to fact-check the predictions, to rate our hopes and worries against their reality.

In this book, for once, the first draft of history is a look ahead.

Save Time and Stamps

Marvin Sirbu

With Madelyn Ross, *Pittsburgh Post-Gazette*

Dr. Marvin Sirbu, formerly with the Sloan School of Management at MIT, holds a joint appointment in engineering and business at Carnegie Mellon University where he's been teaching and writing for the past eight years. His primary interest is in telecommunications policy.

On Usage of Time

All studies show that people have increased the amount of time they spend at work. There's less time for discretionary activities. And if you look at the forecasts of sales and usage of computer games, home computers, VCRs and so on, those items will take up the little discretionary time they have. In a future information age, the hard problem will be how to allocate time.

More and more people will be buying from catalogs. There's no time for me to go shopping during the day, for instance, so I shop from nine to eleven P.M. using the phone and my computer. Estimates right now are that 20 percent of all retail sales come from catalogs. Eight hundred (800) numbers and computers make the cost of ordering low, and as more computers come along, there will be more price competition in catalog buying since computers allow me to price compare. Because of that, all pricing will be on a national market, rather than a local market.

Up until recently, the communications technology really didn't save a lot of time. Paying bills by phone, for instance, was an absurd idea. Telephone pushbuttons cost time. And videotext material was more painful to read than paper, and you were always waiting for it to paint the next screen of type. But computers are getting faster, modems are higher speed, and "point and click" user interfaces are available. Suddenly, I can pay my bills and save both stamps and time.

The widespread use of portable telephones and handheld computers will keep you in touch with the community while you're doing something else—like sitting on the beach with your family. And because we'll have video telephony in 20 years, "my community" won't be restricted by geography.

The Workplace

Because we're working in the competition of a global market, everyone is working longer and longer hours. And because a much larger portion of the population is in the work force and everyone spends off-work time cooking, doing laundry, and so on, everyone will feel even more pressured. The future will be a series of very intense work periods followed by sabbaticals. Because of electronic communications, the whole tempo of business is speeded up. In the past, if a colleague wanted to ask me a question, he or she would put it in the mail. Two days later I'd get it and answer it when I could. But now E-mail interrupts me with an urgency I didn't feel before. Now, I answer immediately and the communication is rapid. It will become more and more difficult to plan your work day; you'll be constantly reallocating your time. This contributes to the sense of pressure and the feeling of not having enough time.

More and more women will enter the work force, and it will become much more difficult to transfer an employee.

For that reason, we'll see more rootedness in a place than in the last few decades.

On Journalism

Print journalism that always found a niche in community coverage, like high school football games, will face a new challenge. With five hundred channels of television available as a result of new technology, programmers will be scratching for things to fill up the time. They'll turn to broadcasting high school football games. Because they must fill those channels, you'll be able to get a lot more community news by television than ever before.

There's already emerging competition over who will build the set-top computer that will manage the menu for five hundred channels.

In-depth coverage will move to weekly magazines. Now we have a lot of reporters writing essentially the same story—take a presidential news conference, for instance. One thing we'll see is less redundancy but the same number of national and world stories covered. What will suffer is the story of corruption in a mayor's office because that story won't sell outside the community and there might not be enough journalism interest in the community to support it. Community journalism is jeopardized.

The proliferation of computer bulletin boards is another challenge. Information travels quickly on them. When there were interruptions with the telephone service around the country last year, the news media was reporting it as a great mystery. But within minutes, technicians were explaining the problem on the bulletin boards.

Because bulletin boards are accessible to anyone, we may see a lot of unprofessional journalism crop up: Joe Smith's sports report, for instance. There will be more low-budget cottage reporting.

American Society of Newspaper Editors

When a Crash Is a Crash!
I kept my cars running for years by knowing how to file down and reset the points in the distributor. (In a pinch, a pop-top would substitute well enough for a point gauge to get you started.) Now cars don't have distributors, and even though I've never had a bit of trouble with electronic ignitions, I've lost a little bit of that sense of security I once had. If anything does go wrong, there's nothing I can do about it. Those wonderful gizmos that are running our houses and our routines will also break down, and cause great disruption whenever they do.

For Art's Sake, Folks!

Helen Vendler

With Jack Driscoll, *The Boston Globe*

Helen Vendler is the A. Kingsley Porter University Professor in the Department of English at Harvard University, from which she received her doctorate in English and American literature. Her previous degree studies were at Emmanuel College, the University of Louvain and Boston University. She is a renowned author, principally on the subjects of poetry and theater, and has served on several prestigious national and international cultural boards.

The arts are going to wither and die in fifteen years if no one teaches them, which is what is happening now in most public schools for reasons of money. There is hardly any serious teaching of singing, drawing and instrument playing. People have to take music lessons on their own; most school orchestras have folded. Howard Gardner of Project Zero at Harvard has argued that there are many different kinds of intelligence and that we should reward and train musical and visual intelligence as well as verbal and mathematical. Education is obliged to facilitate the best development of every child. As things now stand absolutely nothing is done for the visually and musically talented in the first twelve years of public school. That's a great waste of talent and training.

Nobody sings anymore. The Shakers had very much a

musical culture. The Moravians brought a notable musical achievement, but then it died. If children sang in school every day for twelve years, then they would come out not only musically literate but also poetically literate. The schools do singing for the little ones, but then they drop it.

The arts haven't really had very much of a past in this country. In Europe you see some artifact of a thousand-year past every time you turn around. People go to school in old buildings or pass by them in France or Germany or Japan. Here we pass by gas stations and modern buildings. There's a vastly insufficient patriotism of our American culture. Children leave high school without ever having seen an American painting, without ever having heard an American piece of music.

There hasn't been a national core curriculum here as there has been in other countries. Teachers need standards they can then add individually to. It's too politically explosive for the government to focus on content. A real push should be made for a real K–12 curriculum in American national culture. It would be like apple pie and the flag. You'd have to be for it.

We need to become proud of ourselves as a culture. For a long time we deferred to Europe, and rightly so. Then American artists began to flex their muscles, during the period of international modernism, when America emerged as a world power from 1912 to 1960. We had lots of immigrants coming over to fertilize the culture. Worshiping Russian ballet from afar is very different from having Balanchine in your midst.

It takes quite a long time for the trickle-down effect of cultural perception. In England, look at the pride they take in the glory of English literature, English music, English architecture. This type of pride hasn't filtered down to public consciousness here. Newspapers certainly could help by doing more on culture locally and regionally.

The all-day school will eventually be in vogue, because the community will have to support women in the workplace by taking on more functions of the home. The Putney School, where my son attended, is a model for the use of adolescent energy. He got up in the morning and tended to the animals in the barn. If you had animals in schools, all the children would have something to love. (If you have to take care of them, you love them more.) Then they went to breakfast, and everybody learned to cook for the whole school. They did yard work, they cleared ski trails, they made maple syrup, butter, bread. In the evening they had the arts, so they were singing madrigals or off making silver jewelry. By the time they got to bed, they were wonderfully tuckered out.

Indeed, schools should be open twenty-four hours a day. It would be good for high school kids who have after-school jobs to be able to come back at night and study at a study hall, for instance, with somebody there to help them with their algebra. What parent knows algebra any longer? Students could swim or work out or study. School should be a place they should love to come to for many reasons.

Schools can't be expected to take on all the emotional responsibilities of the mother or the father or the grandparent, although I think it's better to have teachers who are fond of their students than otherwise. We're not encouraged as a culture to be fond of our students. We need to know them as people rather than as performers in algebra. One of the nicest things that happened to me was when I was teaching night school at Boston University. We had 180-minute sessions but only 150 minutes of instruction. A break was built in. We all went down and got a Coke and sat at tables and talked to each other like human beings. I latched onto those students more than the ones who come for the daytime lecture, then leave. The schools should have a built-in talk period.

Children should be paid to go to school in some way. I don't know whether it should be by merit or by what system, but look at it this way: 90 percent of the people of the world wouldn't go to work if they weren't paid. An incentive system could be devised to pay children for every single day they go to school at all levels.

It strikes me that the ethnic tribalism that exists in Europe and here is going to have to change. How long can we effectively have ghettos for immigrants? We can't. It's very, very painful to watch in my own city where things have gone too far. I used to do typing summers for the Civil Service around 1948–49. There was one black woman in my office, a college graduate. She was far better educated than the other women in the office. She ate a brown-bag lunch at her desk, all alone, every day. None of the other coworkers would speak to her.

I used to talk to her all the time, and she was quite interesting. The others' isolation of her was so irrational! It upset me. And neither the politicians nor the church nor the schools were very forthcoming on race in Boston. There was no leadership.

Prioritizing has to go on throughout this changeover so that the poor will not be left out. There are no national groups to do anything for the poor, as far as I can see. None at all. The rest of us are exactly in the position of the "good Germans" when the Jews were being carted off. I feel very helpless with respect to what I'm able to do. The schools should have real chairs and real lounges and real listening rooms and real art rooms and real courts, tennis courts and football fields. They should be like colleges. It doesn't have to cost a fortune. There are creative ways. You can get retired people to teach. If people retire at fifty-five, put them in schools till they're eighty. They'd do a lot of work, and it wouldn't cost that much. It would give them all a place to go, and children to be interested in. Every carpenter and pipe fitter in America could be in school teaching kids useful skills.

Every culture is remembered by what it produced in art and learning. It is very rarely remembered for the wars it fought. We ought to look ahead to see how America will be remembered.

On the Future of the Media

I think the electronic explosion is terrific. When I went to school, your education was restricted to the remarks of the individual teacher. When my son went to school, he took out videos for all sorts of things. He came home from the fourth grade and said, "I saw the childbirth tape . . . gross!" Nobody explained childbirth to me in the fourth grade. The teacher is no longer a limiting factor in learning. Independent learning programs will allow students to go deeper and deeper as they wish. I see this opening things up enormously to students who live far from libraries or far from very good teacher training. All schools will have video labs.

As an education device, the split screen in television is interesting. Also the instant replay in slow motion, especially for those who study dance. People will have videophones, because they want to see their grandchildren in California and vice versa.

There will always be computer types calling everything up on screens and people who hate to be in front of a screen. My ideal would be an infrared wire that you could sit with on the couch and essentially turn the pages electronically. You would not have to sit imprisoned in front of the screen. I think a book-format newspaper would be nice. You could sit and run through it electronically, like micro-reading. You could skip pages if you wanted to, you could say 'jump to' and skip a whole section. In every room there will be a socket for receiving electronics, so you can click on your own newspaper the way you click on a radio.

Tahlequah Revisited

Wilma Mankiller

With Ed Kelley, *The Daily Oklahoman*

Wilma Mankiller for seven years has been principal chief of the Cherokee Nation of Oklahoma, the second largest Indian tribe in the United States. Born at the Indian Hospital in Tahlequah, Okla., she became active in Indian causes in the San Francisco area in the 1960s. She took on her present position in 1985 when the chief resigned and was elected the first woman in the position two years later.

A graduate of the University of Arkansas, she lives with her husband, Charlie Soap, in rural Adair County and has two daughters.

More protection for the environment. A better economy. Technology that could keep more Americans in rural areas. And a public education system that will be pressured to make big changes to keep the nation competitive.

That's a look at what life in these United States can be like after the first decade of the next century, if we work hard to be creative and put our collective vision to work.

I admit I am an optimist, not just for the twenty-first century, but for the immediate future. People have always said that, but I have always been proven right.

As the leader of the nation's second-largest Indian tribe, I live near Tahlequah, Okla. It is a small community (population 10,398), not unlike most of the communities of the woodsy hills of northeastern Oklahoma, where many members of my tribe live.

But I envision the day when residents of our region—Native American or not—can take advantage of more of the benefits of the nation's cities without their accompanying problems of crime, traffic and pollution.

For example, we could have a library here with these new CD-ROM computer links that we are just now learning about. We could have a full-fledged international library right here in Tahlequah that would take up very little space.

Using such tools will make life better in the year 2010, when my thirteen-year-old stepson, Winterhawk, is thirty. Here are some other things I see occurring between now and then:

- There will be more attention being paid to preserving the environment.
- I hope our economy will be healthier. And either we are going to be in a world of trouble with public education, or it is going to have to be dramatically changed for us to move forward.
- I am not sure how I feel about reversing the trend and masses of people moving back to rural areas. I think there will be some reversal of that trend; I don't know whether it will be complete.
- And if the technology continues to change to allow people to do a lot of work in their homes as it has done in the last decade, we will see quite a bit of change. But that is difficult to predict.

To help Winterhawk and his generation reach a better life style, we first must have an overhaul of the public school system.

The schools are like huge bureaucracies in 1993. What happens is that the school systems expect the students to adapt to the school system, but the school systems do not adapt to changing populations and a changing world economy. I do not think many of the schools have changed to meet the needs of our country's diverse population.

I think that also is true with regard to the world we are

entering. At this point, most of the schools do not clearly understand how dramatically the world of work has changed in the last decade and where we are headed for the twenty-first century.

Certainly intellectual and technical skills will be valued much more in the twenty-first century than they are now. Far too many school systems view themselves within the context of their communities, and not globally.

I have a sense, though this may be overrated, that students in Japan and some other countries are trained in the public school systems to understand they are a component of a world economy. And when they leave school, they are going to have to know an awful lot about what is going on in the world in general in order to compete. I am not sure we do that in this country.

Like many leaders in the Southwest, I worry, too, about the flight from small towns to big cities and what it has done to the rural landscape. It is particularly true in Oklahoma, my native state, where most of the state's population resides in and around the two metropolitan areas—Oklahoma City and Tulsa.

I think the trend will reverse somewhat over the next decade or so, but only to a certain degree. And it certainly won't happen without enormous efforts.

One thing is for sure: We are not going to see a reversal of that trend until we see more jobs in rural areas. Among the Cherokee people, we began to see a reversal of that trend because we have created jobs. As we have built clinics and built Cherokee Nation industries, people now have a job to come home to.

It is going to take a huge effort, some support from lots of different areas, and lots of different sectors of society to reverse the trend. But the trend is all dependent on the building of an economy.

With the jobs to the cities, of course, go people, many of the type of people who used to be the pillars of our small towns.

Certainly we don't have the kind of people we'd like to have here. In a way, it is a catch-22. We need leaders so we can reverse the trend, and most of the leaders are in Oklahoma City, Tulsa, and other cities because that's where the jobs are. It is a real problem.

But an even bigger issue in the year 2010 will be the environment. Certainly business and environmental groups must change their collective thinking between now and then.

Environmentalists need to stop thinking that every business is out to destroy the entire planet. And business needs to stop thinking that every environmentalist is a nut. People have to stop pigeonholing each other like that and sit down and begin to talk realistically about what we can do to have both a viable economy and also preserve the environment.

Finally, we must teach people the importance of self-reliance, whether it be in Oklahoma or in Washington, D.C. It is a topic I preach constantly at the Cherokee Nation, where our tribe remains on an ambitious economic development program that is now well into its second decade.

Self-reliance—whether in tribes, communities or individuals—will only increase in the next decade and a half.

With self-reliance also comes the ability to articulate your own vision of things, and not buy somebody else's vision. And once people get a taste of that, they are not going to be passive recipients of programs and messages thought up somewhere else, either in Tahlequah or Washington.

Farewell to Workaholism

Linda Chapin

With Jane Healy, *Orlando Sentinel*

Linda Chapin, fifty-one, was a successful banker and active in the League of Women Voters before deciding to run for office in Orlando County, Fla. She was elected to the County Commission in 1986 and four years later became chairman, the most powerful elected position in the Orlando metropolitan area. A graduate of Michigan State, she is married and the mother of four children.

I believe that in twenty years we will have more free time than now because technology will take us in that direction. There will always be workaholics but, increasingly there will be a working climate that doesn't demand as much time as now. If people try to do as much then as technology will allow, they will go crazy. Instead, we will learn as a human race how to make technology work to our advantage.

I also believe that people will want more time with their families, with men much more sensitized to spending time with children. They will have to do so if they want the family unit to work.

I also think there will be efforts in the black community to reestablish the family. Most of all, there will be a backlash against the increasing tolerance for such things as unwed motherhood.

Recreation will also change drastically. In fact, the definition of recreation will have changed so dramatically that it will be almost unrecognizable. It will still involve things like team sports such as Little League, but more attention will be paid to outdoor recreation, to families doing things together and to individual adventure. Maybe there will even be a national bike trail.

As far as transportation overall is concerned, I had thought the transportation system was going to see dramatic changes by now because of technology. But I am less optimistic about that because of the lack of money available for that.

For example, I don't think there will be a magnetically levitated train in Orlando by the year 2000. I do think, however, that we will see a lot more mass transit in some form—maybe in the form of more buses.

I also see cities being revived, with urban cores becoming more important. People spent the last twenty years moving to suburbs. Now they will spend the next twenty making the urban core more attractive.

As far as education, I find the potential change in this area the "scariest one of all." Most important, I have seen tremendous change in the level of dissatisfaction by parents, students, and teachers. They see that there is an inability to make schools work. I believe that schools are a reflection of a larger society. Only in the last decade have they started to fall apart. For one thing, we have bunched kids all together into one mainstream, rather than separating them into different paths, such as college prep and vocational. A very obvious and easy way to improve schools is to back away from that mainstreaming. We need to stress to children the value of their own potential, even if they do not attend college.

One area in which I hold an optimistic view is the environment. People care about it and are speaking out, with an enhanced appreciation for green space and habitat. I think that will carry over in the next twenty years.

American Society of Newspaper Editors

As far as the future of the media, I consider newspapers recreation. I am concerned, though, whether, in twenty years, anyone is going to be reading anything. I wonder whether people will value in-depth information. I don't think television can fill the fourth-estate role very well. I think we'll come back again and people will return to reading.

I believe the media will see more and more specialization and I view newspapers as the carriers of common culture. I think they are incredibly important in that role. But, unfortunately, twenty years from now, the newspaper will be a TV screen, offering the information through that vehicle rather than through newsprint.

The Demise of Rummaging

I hate this, but I expect to see the end of printing on paper as a widespread medium in my lifetime. If recording, duplicating and disseminating information is the ultimate goal, there is hardly any need for paper now. But the ways we access information do have something to do with how we handle it. One of my favorite ways of generating ideas was to rummage randomly through the card catalog system at the public library. Now that it's been replaced by a computer system, the fun and inspiration is hard to come by. In order to find something, you have to know what you're looking for. To me this represents change of a fundamental sort. I think it may affect people's imaginations and their ability to form points of view. The things that I accidentally come across are the things I value most.

Reinventing the West

Donald E. Worster

With Prof. John C. Ginn,
University of Kansas

Dr. Donald E. Worster, Hall Distinguished Professor of American History, University of Kansas, is widely known for his research of the environmental history of North America. A graduate of Yale University and the University of Kansas, he is the author of eight books on the history of the environment, including The Wealth of Nature: Environmental History and the Ecological Imagination *(Oxford University Press, 1993). He has served as president of the American Society for Environmental History and is on the board of directors of the Land Institute and Kansas Land Trust.*

America's environmental-resources paradox likely still will be with us through the first decade of the coming century. Our past behavior and current circumstances suggest that we will continue to be world leaders in our inclination to voice concerns for and to pass legislation that addresses environmental problems. The same evidence suggests that we will continue to cling to the deep-seated cultural attitudes and behaviors that also make us world leaders as wasters of environmental resources.

To date we have not shown much willingness to harness the political will to restrain waste, and I see nothing on the horizon that convinces me that our political will is likely

Come the Millennium

to change dramatically. Some among us might point to the recent decision to increase the tax on gasoline by four cents a gallon and suggest that this is a surge of newfound willingness to sacrifice. However, the truth is that this increase will be painless for most Americans. Indeed, in the past decade or so the price of gasoline often has been far above the level to which the new tax is to take it.

While we are not likely to have leaped forward by the year 2010 in solving the array of environmental problems with which we live, there are some areas where I believe important progress will have been made. Areas of likely progress are the challenges associated with fossil fuels and with global atmospheric change. Nuclear energy is not likely to be part of this progress. That technology seems to be going nowhere in the 1990s. And solar energy has lost so much momentum that it is not likely to be delivering important parts of the solution in the next twenty years. However, we are likely to make substantial progress in having autos that get gas mileage of something like ninety miles to the gallon. Actually the technology to do this exists in 1993, though it is not yet economically viable. It is noteworthy that the Japanese are likely to be the engineers, manufacturers, and marketers of this high-mileage technology. An especially encouraging American development is the progress we have made in the mid-1990s with ozone depletion. The reversal of this depletion trend is heartening for the world, and it is evidence that the U.S. leadership in an area can make a difference. We need to recognize, however, that the global-warming trend is a more complex problem.

The scarcity of water resources will be a much greater environmental issue for Americans in 2010. That will be especially true for those living in the western states. I expect this water-resource-driven economic dislocation to be as big a transition in this country as the military downsizing that is currently under way. There will be dramatic cutbacks in the land available for agricultural uses, because much of the water that irrigates that land today will have been diverted to meet the demands of urban industrial and residential areas. Today there are states where 85 to 90 percent of the water resources are devoted to agriculture. That kind of water-use allocation will not be sustainable two decades from now. I do not expect that change to threaten our food supply. Much of that water today goes to cattle raising, and we do seem to be changing our eating habits in ways that make our diets less dependent on beef. The western United States—a boom area of this country for more than one hundred years—will have to reinvent itself because of this revolutionary shift in the use and availability of water.

A reasonable generalization is that we are learning much about the science of solving environmental problems we have created. Are we learning enough to keep up with the new environmental problems we are creating? My sense is that we are at least putting our finger in the dike for now and for a few generations. I am more optimistic now than I was ten years ago. But at some point we almost certainly will have to make some life-style adjustments that yield important conservation results.

A Scam on Ourselves

Ron Crouch

With Timothy M. Kelly, *Lexington (Ky.) Herald-Leader*

Ron Crouch is director of the Kentucky State Data Center, a federal-state cooperative headquartered at the University of Louisville that acts as an information clearinghouse for the Census Bureau and other data sources. He holds a bachelor's degree from Kentucky Southern College, two master's degrees from the University of Louisville in sociology and social work, and an MBA from Bellarmine College. He is or has been active in health and welfare reform, homeless issues, and the Sierra Club.

The country has one major issue. It's not welfare, not education, not work force, and not diversity.

It's an aging society and how we deal with it. That is the real issue driving most of the country but nobody wants to talk about it. It's simply too touchy.

Americans in their fifties, sixties, and seventies are the most well-off generation this country has ever seen, and they had better start growing up. They've had it easy. They worked hard, but they also lucked out. Their parents didn't luck out, and their children and grandchildren aren't doing nearly as well as they've done.

Their money and income are dominating the culture. About 80 percent of all money in bank accounts now is held by people fifty-five or over. And yet, we are bankrupting our country's future with the spending on Social Security and Medicare and Medicaid, which are becoming the Pac-Men of our budget.

Twenty years from now people who are in their twenties and thirties could be paying just an enormous share of their gross wages to the government.

More and more people are going to have to pay for an aging society and won't have enough money to buy houses, cars, books, whatever. It's very much the same for the business community. There will be less money to invest in business production. We'll be moving money from productive resources to unproductive resources.

We're putting money into the past at the expense of the future. Basically, we're running a big scam—a scam on the future—and that's going to be the big problem.

We need to awaken America to this issue. And we have to convince people they will have to work longer because they are living longer.

When Social Security was established in 1935, life expectancy was sixty-three and retirement age was sixty-five. And the system worked very well.

Today, life expectancy is seventy-six, but 68 percent of the population already takes early retirement at age sixty-two. So we're actually living thirteen years longer and retiring about three years sooner. It is an issue the public and the politicians are going to have to face.

This country would not be growing if it were not for our growing older. The only real growth is in the population thirty-five and over.

Just as an example, consider this: In 1990, 36,000 people in the United States were one-hundred-plus. People now in their early sixties will reach the age of one hundred near 2030. The Census Bureau projects in the year 2030 that those one-hundred-plus will have increased from 36,000 to 435,000—a twelvefold increase.

And for those of us who are older boomers, born in the late 1940s, the Census Bureau is estimating that 1,170,000 will reach one-hundred-plus.

Come the Millennium

The good news is we're living a lot longer. The bad news is we're living a lot longer.

It used to be the average person lived 7 percent of his or her lifetime in retirement. That figure is now approaching about a quarter of the lifetime. The average person now lives eighteen years beyond retirement.

We can plan for the future we want, or we can plan for the future we're going to get. If we can bring them close together, that's fine. But if they're far apart and it's not realistic, then we've got real problems.

The Social Security system would have been bankrupt a long time ago if not for the huge increase of women in the work force. In 1991, $269 billion—nearly one-fourth of the federal budget—went to Social Security payments. Another $57 billion went to federal employment retirement, and $184 million went to Medicare and Medicaid.

So, we need to change from disabling people to enabling people. Right now we have a system that tries to disable people as soon as possible rather than enabling people and keeping them working as long as possible, and being effective as long as possible.

People should retire when they become old and disabled, not just because they have reached a particular age.

Likewise, we need to redefine the whole issue of education. We've got to stop thinking about education as grades K–12 and start thinking of education as going from K through eighty. We have to have lifelong learning, retooling, retraining. That's going to be the issue of education in the future: constantly making your work force productive.

The best social security will be a skilled, educated lifestyle that allows us to continue working and continue to be productive.

The question for newspapers, then, is what does this aging population mean?

Certainly, it means newspapers need to make the print bigger. That's the easy part.

Beyond that, newspapers can have scenarios both negative and positive depending on whether we continue to disable people at fifty-five or sixty. If we decide to enable people to keep them involved longer, engaged longer, educated longer, then it is a totally different scenario. I hope we will take the latter.

Newspapers have a dilemma. I hear that your readership wants to get its stories good and quick and doesn't want to have to think too much about it, or analyze it.

The choice seems to be between trying to educate the readership generally, by giving people a little glimpse with no substance, like the *USA Today* format. Or do we want an educated society, with the real detail that is needed to help make real decisions?

When I look at data and trends, it seems to me that newspapers need to be giving out more information and more detail, not less information and less detail.

We are going to have to become a society that thinks more and makes hard choices, one that prioritizes more. And that means we have to have a better-educated population, not a more entertained population.

The Techno Backlash

Craig J. Thompson

With Frank Denton, *Wisconsin State Journal*

Craig J. Thompson is an assistant professor of business at the University of Wisconsin–Madison. At age thirty-one, he already is winning national visibility as a theorist in marketing. A native of Knoxville, Tenn., he graduated in 1984 then earned his Ph.D. in 1991 at the University of Tennessee at Knoxville. His dissertation was on consumer-satisfaction experiences of married professional women. His primary areas of interest are gender issues in consumption, post-modern research techniques, and the effect of media images on self-concept.

Four overarching forces are changing the American lifestyle and psyche quickly and profoundly. They undoubtedly are interrelated, in complex ways; their implications certainly are.

The first is the pressure to be productive, with people being swept up by time constraints and technology. This was supposed to be the dawning of the Age of Leisure—remember that? We worried about what would people do with all the leisure time created by shorter work weeks and labor-saving appliances. But instead, there is a universal feeling of time poverty. Deborah Schor addressed that in her book, *The Overworked American.* One of the persuasive messages that consumers have been given, over and over, is buy this for the convenience, for saving time. But it has been documented that these things have not created more leisure time; they just increase the demand. The more things you have, the more things you have to take care of. I'm not convinced that even the microwave oven has saved us time. My dissertation got into that area. For working women, the microwave simplifies cooking, but it also brings with it guilt, from not preparing food. And it breaks down the meal ritual, the social setting. I don't want to romanticize the pre-microwave days, but the old way did require us to take a break and sit down together.

We think we control technology, but in fact, it is technology that tends to control us. Look at fast food: We're hearing now that seven seconds for the delivery of fast food is too slow. There is a sense that everything has to be done quickly.

Research by the Prodigy and on-line shopping-network people shows that people despise shopping, even though they do a lot of it. So if they can phone and have things delivered, they will. But they still grocery-shop; why? It may be a time out, when I can stop running. I don't even mind standing in line. Taking time to do something is enjoyment, a break.

We've got to get out of always increasing productivity, always being more productive every minute. That's what is promoted in advertising: You've got to do this more quickly, it's a dog-eat-dog world. The message is: "If you have this new technology, something good awaits you," but in the end, it's just more technology.

I think there will be a backlash, a new social trend, toward a simpler life-style. It's small now, but it's cutting edge. People will want more quality of life.

The second force is more political, a growing sense of class distinction, people wanting to seize more power. You see it in the grassroots movement to stop NAFTA, but it's indicative of a larger trend. People are beginning to wonder, to think that globalization may lower our standard of living. We have been told that, because of globalization, we have to work harder, and that's not going over very well.

Come the Millennium

There is a growing sense of class distinction, of unfair concentrations of wealth. People are becoming more aware and wanting to take action.

The public didn't react badly to Bill Clinton's two-hundred-dollar haircut just because that's not what a president should do; it touched a nerve because it showed a class distinction.

News reports tend to take the upper-class view, glorifying consumption. The media don't link consumer trends and needs with economic issues. Perot does, and so do some of the fringe elements, like skinheads, and that's why they have some degree of success with the public.

There is a much greater motivation for people to want to control politics and government. That was part of the appeal of Jerry Brown in the 1992 campaign. People are tired of being pacified; they want change.

It ties back to the life style point. People are reacting negatively to marketing images, the bimbo beer ads. There is an excluding of marginalized groups, like women and minorities. It's similar to the beginning of the civil rights movement, but it's more complex, because the groups are. Everyone is becoming more sophisticated about these issues, not just intellectual circles.

All of this is leading to emotion and hostility against the mainstream media. The media aren't connecting and reflecting these people's experiences and perspectives very well. Stories are always written from the perspective of the officials, the power elite. Issues are framed by them. People want to see more of their perspective in the newspaper.

People have changed, but their media have not.

The third force is environmental consciousness. Even companies are using this as a promotional strategy. Wal-Mart is spending twice as much on its stores to show its commitment to the environment. It's a concentrated effort in business sectors.

The catch is that, in a consumption-driven society like ours, you have to have "economic growth," which means more and more consumption, more retailers, more demand for fuel and raw materials. This represents two competing forces: a desire for more responsibility versus ever-expanding growth. These are both structural factors that are meeting increasingly head-on. It is becoming more difficult to ignore these environmental issues.

This is all embedded in the ecological system, so how do you get the economy to live in harmony with environmental consciousness? Recycling is not enough. We accept GM's layoffs to "become more competitive," but we won't accept layoffs to save the spotted owl. We have to reconcile these conflicts.

We will have to decide whether to reclaim the inner cities rather than cut down a forest to build a new shopping center. We'll have to live in closer proximity to each other.

The other force is a general sense that the American dream is becoming less applicable to people's daily lives, that is, a good job, a secure old age, children who will live better than their parents. We're feeling very threatened, powerless. People aren't seeing a lot of leadership, from the politicians or the media.

In the context of history, the American dream was more of a myth anyway. Through major social movements, women's suffrage, the socialist movement, the violent union movement, and then in the 1940s and 1950s, the country developed a social net, and growth extended to more people, though many still were excluded. Now, globalization and the loss of power of the unions have undercut those improvements. Workers feel they have less control. They have a pretty good intuitive sense of social forces over the last ten years in this regard.

These forces are not systematically addressed in the mainstream media, just sporadically. There is a complex network of interrelated factors, but we tend to break out pieces to analyze and argue about. We need to understand the larger dynamic. Clinton wants to talk in a more holistic sense, but people feel overwhelmed by the enormity of it all, so they accuse him of "a lack of focus." Little issues can undercut the big ones. People need to be led to look at the bigger picture and see the connections. There is so much implicit framing, and that can have a tremendous impact on public perceptions.

With desktop publishing and the new technology, people will see more media.

As for mainstream newspapers, people believe that, because of economic pressures, there is less real reporting going on, less talking to real people and more use of official sources. The media are really serving less of a critical, reflective role and showing more views of the people in power.

Media conglomerates are leading to less of an incentive for media to challenge the status quo.

Newspapers should show how this is going to affect me, what are real people feeling and thinking and doing. We need more coverage of grass-roots movements like those I've talked about. You need to make these movements more credible and meaningful. Instead, news events are framed as events outside anyone's control, or at least the average person's control. Newspapers should show people: "I can have some sort of control over this."

American Society of Newspaper Editors

Of Gadgets and Gizmos
Our houses are already quite high-tech environments, and soon they will be filled with gadgets and gizmos that run themselves and are really neat and really take care of a lot of our needs, as well as providing unthought-of forms of amusement. These things also are increasingly dictating the way we do things. If we program the damned things to minister to our needs on a certain schedule, we become slaves to that schedule. The device owes loyalty only to its maker and will cheerfully perform in ways it knows would make its designer proud. If the designer has different notions of how you should be doing something than you do, guess who makes the necessary changes.

A Recipe for Yecch

Amr Ismail

With Lou Ureneck, The Portland, Maine, Newspapers

Dr. Amr Ismail is a horticulturist and internationally known expert in the field of blueberry cultivation. He has combined his plant science background with an entrepreneurial spirit to put Maine Wild Blueberry Co. at the top of its field as a supplier to such companies as Burger King, Procter and Gamble, Kraft General Foods, and Ben and Jerry's. Born in Egypt, Dr. Ismail now lives in Machias, Maine, where he is the president and CEO of Maine Wild Blueberry Co.

You are going to see major changes in agriculture, whether it's wild blueberries, beef, or vegetables. The changes will come from genetic manipulation and the technology of tissue culture. You will see better tomatoes and chickens that lay more eggs. These techniques are going to result in better quality, better shelf life, better flavor, more resistance to disease, better uniformity, better ripening, longer shelf life, and a reduction in cost. Increases in production through genetic engineering will be routine.

Other major changes will be much less reliance on pesticides because of their impact on the environment, cost, and social awareness. Genetic engineering will offer alternatives to pesticides through development of resistant plant material and pests that feed on pests.

I envision changes in food to meet the population. This may sound like "yecch," but there is an outstanding source of protein and nutrition in this world. It is insects. They are food now in Latin America and Africa. People already eat grasshoppers, larvae of ants, crickets. What is lobster but an insect? Insects could be cultivated, grown, and managed in huge quantities on the assembly line. The only thing radical is the limitations of our thinking.

There has been a lot of technological change of food processing. People in this country are resisting food irradiation. This should stop. It is safe, practical, economical, energy efficient, and sound. There would be less disease and better health for the consumer.

There is going to be more technology in food processing. The product will be loaded onto a truck or railroad car through a hose, a button will be pushed which will be the last human contact until the product is baked or frozen and shipped.

Consumer expectations are going to change. They will want a more perfect product, a more consistent and uniform product. More technology, more specialized machinery, more computer systems—all of this will require more technical training of people and higher capital investment. There will be more production but less margin per unit.

There are going to be more restrictions in the workplace. More standardization, more regulation on health and hazards, on air quality temperature, and on behavior in the workplace. More government in every aspect of the workplace as it chases those elusive qualities, fairness and equality, and that means less individualism and creativity. The workplace will be more demanding.

Competition will be stiffer. Business will move to where the profitability is. As we get more competition, there will have to be more systems that reduce waste. Waste is a very major liability. One of the best systems to reduce waste is to manufacture a product right the first time. No scrap. This is the whole concept of Deming: Having a capable and robust process.

There have got to be real changes in how business is

done. The whole concept is wrong of CEOs with short-term thinking: arrive at a company, hit hard, get big salaries, shuffle the cards, then leave to have the company picked by another corporation, only to have it fall apart. This must change. There must be more continuity, less making money on paper. Global competition will make it change. There must be and will be less reliance on quarterly profits and annual earnings. The important thing in business is satisfaction of the customer.

People on the line will have to have much better reading and math skills, much better reasoning skills in which they take what they know in pieces and make a sentence and structure a decision out of it.

There will be more training in technical skills and computer logic, then training for special applications. Things are going to be more complicated than they are right now. People have got to get the basics and beyond. How it is going to be done, I don't know. But it must. People are an important part of the process.

Take Me to "Heaven"

Robert H. Thibadeau

With Madelyn Ross, *Pittsburgh Post-Gazette*

Dr. Robert H. Thibadeau is the senior research scientist at The Robotics Institute of Carnegie Mellon University. He has developed a paradigm for predicting the future by following current trends to their natural conclusions. He is currently developing computer television which would attach (or build in) a computer to all television sets.

On Transportation

Transportation will move into space. It will be automatic transport. We'll get into something and simply say "Hong Kong" and the transportation system will get us there.

On Manufacturing

Manufacturing will move away from goods and into services. For instance, we won't be buying staplers from a company anymore; we'll buy a stapling service. We'll actually buy the right to have the most current stapler which will be delivered to us. This trend has already begun in the car lease business.

On Social Revolutions

A system of private trusts will handle most of our social needs, much like private insurance companies are moving to handle all health-care needs. We'll buy into various trusts that will provide services to us.

Taxes will be eliminated and an invisible financing system will be developed to support public needs so that through our work government mechanisms are automatically funded. I don't know exactly how it will work, but some guy will figure out a system where, if I buy something that costs a dollar, I'll give the merchant plastic money which magically changes into sixty cents. We'll never have to pay taxes again and no one can cheat.

On Politics

The telecommunications revolution and the subsequent direct contact between politician and voters will lead to multiple parties or no parties at all. The two-party system will be gone.

On Computers

Computers are already considered to be universal machines and soon everything will be computerized. Everything will be "smart." Any object will do whatever we tell it to, becoming our new slaves. Everything will be simplified further because we'll be able to make machines work by talking at them.

On Telecommunications

Telecommunications will allow instant person-to-person communication. We'll have a little badge or button on our lapels that will allow us to speak to anyone in the world at any moment. This will be followed by "direct-to-brain" communications so we won't even have to speak to make things work—we'll just have to think.

On Business

Capitalism, which is built on a tiering of authority—namely, bosses and workers—will end. Business coalitions will be built for global sales. And the real power will be the power of persuasion and publishing. People who command respect will control business. And if you have an open competition for authority, the person who's trustworthy and truthful will win.

On Newspapers

Newspapers in their current form will coexist with interactive television for a while. But eventually, all information will be conveyed on your television computer, which will sort and distill millions of sources of information. It will get to the point where you'll walk into your living room and say to your television: "You know me by now, tell me what I need to know today." We will have, in essence, customized newspapers produced in our living rooms. Local news staffs will still be gathering and interpreting information, but they won't be producing a news *paper* anymore and all the distribution problems will evaporate. We won't be worrying about how close to the door the newspaper was thrown, you'll be in the TV in the living room.

The Millennial Generation

Stewart Brand

With William German and
Matthew Wilson, *San Francisco Chronicle*

Stewart Brand founded the original Whole Earth Catalog *in 1968 and received the national Book Award for* The Last Whole Earth Catalog. *He then founded* Co-Evolution Quarterly, *now entitled* Whole Earth Review.
In 1984 he began the WELL (Whole Earth 'Lectronic Link), a computer teleconference system for the San Francisco Bay area. In 1986 he was visiting scientist at the MIT Media Laboratory, and in 1988 was cofounder with Peter Schwartz, Jay Oglivy, and others of the Global Business Network.
A prolific author, his books include Two Cybernetic Frontiers *and* The Media Lab: Inventing the Future at MIT.

Chronicle: It seems that everybody in our business is concerned that newspapers are going to be dinosaurs.
Stewart Brand: If television becomes really interactive, more unique, five hundred channels and all that, will newspapers make a big comeback as the only in-common daily news medium? By eschewing interactivity, newspapers win.
Chronicle: Editors are asking, "What are people going to

be like in the next twenty years or so? Are people going to be happy, and why?"

Brand: Global Business Network has been looking at the "happy" question. It opens a peculiar window on the present. Global Business Network—Peter Schwartz and the rest of us—have been traveling the world, talking to corporations and talking to the universes they buy and sell in. The grimness about the future is absolutely *epidemic* and worldwide. Except for bits and pieces of Southeast Asia, which are doing just fine thank you, and get out of our way. Everywhere else has got their head down.

Chronicle: Where is this pessimism coming from? When did it appear?

Brand: It may be like the Clinton administration, in a funny way. Expectations got so understandably inflated, with the demise of the Cold War . . . we've been so used to being afraid of one thing, a kind of a weird, abstract, goony thing, in the way of nuclear confrontation that was going to burn the world down. Then that goes away, and you go "Okay, great! Now this is the 'sunlit uplands' Winston Churchill promised forty-five years ago."

Then that doesn't happen and instead of a nice big simple scary story, you go into an infinity of small but suddenly personally large or grim stories. Somehow we weren't grieved about Lebanon so long as there was the Cold War to kind of put it into context. Now you have Bosnia just going on its own maniacal course—without any context to make sense out of it. And AIDS. . . .

Mood stuff is much larger scale, I think, and more mercurial, because of electronic media, probably. The scary thing to me, is that the Generation X crowd is so pessimistic and basically afraid.

Chronicle: Afraid of what?

Brand: Well, they're still afraid of nuclear war! Doug Coupland's book is wonderful—have you read it?

One of the characters is frantically afraid of radiation and has a whole neurotic behavior around it, which is totally inappropriate now. The environmental stuff I feel mixed feelings about, because people are actually out there thinking that 40 percent of landfill is fast food packaging, or diapers. . . .

A good book to pass around is *Generations*. It's fat, it's journalistic, it's actually somewhat predictive.

They're saying what they call a "thirteener"—now a thirteener is Generation X—is like the silent generation, kind of a downer generation, and that they're going to play out a minor role.

The next bunch coming along is maybe closer to your generation, GIs, who held the White House for thirty years and can take on anything, Gulf War, anything—let's do it!

And "the millennial generation" is how they refer to the one now born, looking at all this probably with growing disgust and dismay. And they come upon some crisis early in the next century which they will be in charge of fixing. A world crisis. And then with the pride based on that, will make the twenty-first century that is competent, confident, and can return to being somewhat happy.

Moods, like fashions, are obliged to shift.

Chronicle: You said earlier that there would probably be come crisis of note in the 2010s or so that the next generation would solve and lead to great optimism.

Brand: It's likely to be close to your business, which is the business and information domain.

Peter Drucker (in *Post Capitalist Society*) says that the radical feminists and the various groups of color and the 'we want our own language' groups are penalizing themselves by wanting their separatist program. Especially in the growing information environment. It is common culture which is being played out. It's worldwide, and it speaks English, and pretty much operates businesses in recognizably the same ways, with important variations in different cultures that can easily be accommodated by the information technology.

Herman Kahn was right (in *The Year 2000*) when he said that computer technology will improve in productivity and efficiency and lower cost at least tenfold every year. He was absolutely dead-on right about that. And what's weird is that forty years later it's still the case.

Chronicle: You're right about the technology improving, but not necessarily the productivity of those who use it.
Brand: Well, that's coming around too. Part of an optimistic scenario now for the economy is that this is starting to play out.
Chronicle: And part of the argument is once PCs are networked, that's when you start to get the productivity.
Brand: I think that's dead-on, the networking. We call it the fax effect. There was a year when faxes were a luxury, and then sort of a year and a half later, faxes were an absolute necessity. You could not be in business without one.

But fax is so obviously an interim technology, and the Internet and ASCII technology is starting to take off.

Networking is a universe that rewards people for being part of it. And eventually when others notice they're being punished for not being part of it, they jump across that line.
Chronicle: Getting back to the communications revolution in the United States: What about advertising?
Brand: Nicholas Negroponte of MIT's Media Lab has a one-liner: You "replace advertising as noise with advertising as news."
Chronicle: The Macy's Channel. . . .
Brand: Something like that. The problem in going to the department store is the company has accumulated experience, shared experience, and you, the customer, are all alone against all that shared experience. On line, you could have the situation where your customers share experience to the same degree that the people who sell the products do, and then you've got a parity which is much better than you've got in the department store.
Chronicle: So you're arguing, almost, that advertising survives if advertising changes its form fairly dramatically.
Brand: Yeah. It can do it. It's interesting. Radio is doing fine. Magazines are doing fine. Basically, the more niche-based they became, the more secure they became. So if anything, we're getting reinforcement of niche commercial behavior in information as in everything else.

Come the Millennium

Chronicle: So what will happen with advertising is the same thing that's happening to the larger culture, the multiculture? It's all niche, there's no mass. That doesn't portend well for the television networks; nor does it portend well for newspapers, which have not been niche publications.
Brand: I think you go both directions. You get both more niche and more overall.
Chronicle: So what happens to multimedia?
Brand: The problem is, the pyramid is inverted. With multimedia, a million person-months of effort have gone into making this exquisite electronic product, and then you stick it in the consumer's hands and he is done with it in an hour. There's got to be a whole lot of people who are going to spend that hour to pay for the man-months.
Chronicle: How do you get enough band width to deliver multimedialike content to the home?
Brand: Band width is funny. These office buildings that wired up with fiber optics—they would have been better off putting in mail chutes. It's just not being used. Maybe there will be a network effect that takes off at some point, but when it does, fiber optic will be unrecognizable. What it's being replaced by is radio frequency—where the door hinges are talking to the wristwatches and the air conditioner.

Band width is doing great across oceans, and competing with satellite transmissions because of the lag question. Fiber-optic cable is getting better and better, so whatever you put in is now going to be obsolete tomorrow.

But we haven't found the killer application yet, where you've got to have broad band or die. But it could come at any time, and then the network effect happens.
Chronicle: Who wins the cable-telephone battle?
Brand: My prediction in *The Media Lab* was both, and I would still make it. For political reasons, the FCC and Congress can't bear to fall on one side or the other of that particular watershed. So, the regulators will let both fight it out. And they'll try to keep the fight equal.

That we don't have an electronic yellow pages is appalling, or even an electronic phone book. There will be an electronic Internet directory, come hell or high water, because the universe will collapse without it. It's so desperately needed. Electronic yellow pages is a great future for somebody, and if I were in the newspaper business I would be making a strategic alliance with telephone companies to do that.

Chronicle: So is it going to be entertainment that drives this revolution?

Brand: That is the widespread assumption.

Personally, I would watch the sex industry—because that's where everything comes first, so to speak.

The book I almost did was called *Outlaws, Musicians, Lovers, and Spies*. It was going to be about the undergrounds that create the markets. Often the technology has grass roots—underground precommercial activity always leads above-ground commercial activity. And you can make millions just by following along one-and-a-half steps behind. . . .

A Library on My Belt

Michael Hooker

With Larry McDermott, *Springfield* (Mass.) *Union-News* and *Sunday Republican*

> *Dr. Michael K. Hooker assumed the presidency of the University of Massachusetts on September 1, 1992. He earned his B.A. degree with highest honors in 1969 at the University of North Carolina at Chapel Hill, where he majored in philosophy. He received his M.A. and Ph.D. from the University of Massachusetts at Amherst in philosophy, and from 1973 to 1975 was an assistant professor in Harvard's department of philosophy.*
>
> *He began his career in administration at The Johns Hopkins University, where he held a variety of posts from 1975 to 1982 which included assistant professor of philosophy, assistant dean, associate dean, and at age thirty-five he became dean of undergraduate and graduate studies. From 1982 to 1986, he was president of Bennington College, Vermont, and from 1986 to 1991 he was president of the University of Maryland, Baltimore County.*
>
> *He lives in Cambridge now and was born in Richlands, Va., on August 24, 1945.*

The twenty minutes in the morning that I read my newspaper and drink my cup of coffee are probably the most precious moments of my day. Nothing else has impinged on me yet, my mind is not on anything else. It's my time. It's a ritual, and it's part of what sustains and preserves my sanity. I mean, I really do love it, and I can't imagine being without it.

In fact, on those rare mornings when the newspaper hasn't shown up, I have gone berserk. I've wanted to kill somebody because my newspaper didn't come.

But, in point of fact, I don't use the newspaper to get my news. I use it for analysis. I already have seen or heard the news. I turn to the newspaper for the editorial-page opinions and to read the analysis of important issues. I know that if there is an important news event, it's history by the time I get my newspaper.

The newspaper is a real anachronism. It is cumbersome to manipulate. When it arrives, the information that it contains is history, not news, and it is presented in such a way that you have to either read a lot that you're not interested in to find what you are interested in, or at least you have to scan through a lot of information before you can zero in on the articles that you're interested in.

Even though much of it is history when it gets to me, I don't think that newspapers are likely to disappear because of this tactile thing, and it's just such a part of the culture, an important part of the culture.

It is not, however, a part of my twelve-year-old daughter's culture. While she reads the newspaper, I don't think many of her contemporaries read it because I've asked her. She says they read the funnies. So, I would guess that the next generation is more attuned to broadcast media, and that when they become conscious of the news, they might be more inclined to get it from broadcast media than from newspapers.

There's probably nothing you can do about that. It's inevitable.

It's best, then, for you to think of yourself as an institution that acquires, processes, and disseminates information than as an institution that prints newspapers.

The provision of that information is a growth industry for the future. Television and radio news don't do a very good job of acquiring, processing or presenting the news.

Most radio news seems to be somebody sitting there reading the stories they have clipped out of the newspaper that morning.

There is a need for high-quality providers of information. They must be institutions that can acquire it, sort it, prioritize it, analyze it, and disseminate it in a form that users want.

Right now, that's exactly what newspapers do.

I see an enormous revolution on the horizon in the way we get our information, and the quality and quantity of information we receive. Each of us is going to become an idiosyncratic, highly personalized receiving node. That will happen with digital broadcasting, so we can get a lot more information into a given span of time. You will find that these receivers are very intelligent.

Within fifteen years, receivers will be programmed with intelligent software so that there will be continuous broadcast, and my car radio will be constantly receiving the articles that I am most interested in. My receiver will be programmed to understand and appreciate my interests.

As soon as I get into the car, it will begin giving me a kind of index, and it will have prioritized them. When I hear a story I'm interested in at that moment, I will interact with the receiver by verbally telling it to play the story in abbreviated form. It will ask if I want more, and if I say yes, it will play more.

If I recall hearing a story on the same subject two weeks prior, I'll ask the receiver to search its database and replay that story.

The same receiver would fit neatly on my belt, as the beeper does, or in a briefcase or purse. Armed with this receiver, I would get updates at any time.

Now, this might sound fantastical, but the computer science department here at the University of Massachusetts has already developed a software that will provide this level of intelligent information retrieval. It's just a question now of being able to imbed this intelligent information retrieval software into a receiver. We will need digital receivers for cars. They aren't here yet, but they are coming.

When we each have a receiver, the news we get will be highly personalized.

Now, it's going to take a big organization to acquire and disseminate this information.

The news industry will be a growth industry. People will pay a premium for getting highly tailored news. It's important that newspapers get into this market early, to make the mistakes, and develop, and move yourself up on the learning curve.

A most interesting question is where advertising fits into this because consumers simply will not be able to afford the service if the provider must pass along all its costs. How advertising becomes a part of the scenario is unknown to me, but I know it will be there because it will be an effective way to reach consumers.

I can envision you being able to hit with pinpoint accuracy very specific market targets for advertisers, and I expect they would pay a real premium for that.

I also think the ads would be much more effective and would be seen more as information. They would provide product information rather than simply product propaganda.

In the realm of being the provider rather than simply a newspaper printer, you could be supplying pedagogical materials for school classrooms with the very same technology and the very same research capacity that you will have available and use in order to supply information to your readers now about what happened over the last twelve hours. What you could do in the future would be a continuous stream. The world will have an even greater appetite for information fifteen years from now.

Of course, we don't know exactly what that world will be like. It baffles me because of the growing bipolarization of the country along the lines of education and income. The middle is disappearing. People are migrating to the poles, where in the one you have the undereducated, though schooled, the underemployed and poor. And at the other end you have folks who are more educated and affluent. The economy is not going to reward people at the lower end.

Come the Millennium

The challenge for you will be perhaps your greatest ever.

As a producer of newspapers, what you must do first is determine how you conceive yourself. Are you an organization that supplies newspapers or are you an organization that supplies information?

Remington and Underwood saw themselves as being in the typewriter business. IBM saw itself as being in the word-processing business. The rest is history.

American Society of Newspaper Editors

Electronic Fishwrap?
Microchips and electronic displays work a fundamental change in everything they touch, but the most dramatic change they affect in the news-delivery system is to make it dependent on the technology. You are not going to wrap fish or line the bird cage or let the kids make crafts projects out of the video terminal after you've finished reading the day's news. We could be losing out on an important cultural link between the recipients because the medium has too much intrinsic value. If newspapers want to continue to be an important presence in people's home, they should think about stuff like that. I think it is important that users can rip out a comic strip and stick it on the refrigerator, or the office bulletin board. The electronic equivalents of the future should have something to fill the same functions. Not necessarily bundling up garbage, but making the "paper" an item that sticks around, continues to get used, and needn't be treated with so much respect.

Make That "Taxamerica"

Arthur W. Orr

With Tom Wright, *Decatur* (Ala.) *Daily*

Arthur Orr, twenty-nine, is an attorney from Decatur, Ala., who received his B.A. in English from Wake Forest University in Winston-Salem, N.C., and his law degree from the University of Alabama in Tuscaloosa. In addition to extensive world travel, he worked from 1989 to 1991 for the U.S. Peace Corps in the Kingdom of Nepal.

Predicting or hypothesizing about the state of our country and world in the year 2015 must be openly acknowledged for what it is—pure speculation and guesswork. With this understanding in mind, I must state that I am generally pessimistic about the future of our country but such pessimism should not be imputed to the world at large. Within the framework of the following topic areas, I'll briefly delineate my thoughts on each: (1) life-style, (2) work and the workplace, (3) transportation, (4) education/culture and (5) environment.

Life-style

The year 2015 will reveal a much more security-conscious populace in the United States. Uniformed armed guards will be more omnipresent in stores, offices, neighborhoods, recreational areas, etc., while neighborhoods might well be sequestered with walls and have only certain monitored points of ingress and egress. In the alternative, high walls around the home might become the rule—similar to present-day upper-class Third World neighborhoods.

I also foresee government at all levels being more powerful and pervasive in everyday life than it is today. I fear that because people cannot properly regulate themselves through honesty and fair dealing, government will be called upon to make more rules and enforce them, which will certainly require more tax dollars. I do not think the Orwellian concept of "Big Brother" will evolve, nor will people see an erosion of their basic civil liberties. But where citizens cannot conduct themselves properly, with handguns for example, the government will have to respond with stringent regulatory measures.

You will find mentioned through this Nostrodamian epistle a recurring reference to higher taxes. The increase of government regulation will require higher tax revenues and will result in the economic polarization of our society. The middle class will be squeezed more and more. Though some will be able to increase their standard of living, most will encounter an economic glass ceiling created by progressive tax rates. The possibility of fulfilling the American dream through hard work will diminish with the passage of time. Incentive will suffer and a malaise of entrepreneurial fervor will occur. Upward mobility will become increasingly rare. As stated below, a larger portion of our populace will not be able to mentally compete at higher levels and will be relegated to low-paying service jobs without much hope of improving their station in life.

Briefly, I believe race relations in the United States will continue to improve among the general population. There will always be, regrettably, extremists among both the majority and minority communities which will have a sizable deleterious effect on the overall populace.

With regard to newspapers, I believe newspapers will

still be a vital part of our lives but home subscriptions will be through a modem and access code. Subscribers will use their remote controls to turn "the pages" on their big screen HDTVs. Hard-copy or paper newspapers will still be published because of their mobility and the failure of older generations to adapt and feel comfortable with a "paperless newspaper."

Overseas, I see the life-styles of foreigners, particularly in Asia, as improving dramatically. I don't necessarily see the United States in a state of decline. I do think our economy and to an even greater extent Europe's are going to be growing at a slower rate than the Asian economy. It is the dawn of mass consumerism in greater Asia outside the already-developed cities and Japan.

Work and the Workplace

Though I alluded to it above, I believe the Asian economy will become the undisputed industrial engine for the world economy, particularly with the conversion of China to a more open economy (albeit a slow conversion). The labor cost *and* skill levels of the Asian worker will cause a serious strain on the manufacturing/industrial sectors of the European and North American economies. Though we will remain the technological leader, the mass production of goods will occur in Asia—let me say, that when I refer to "Asia" I speak roughly of Pakistan eastward.

I believe three primary trading blocks will evolve, one comprised of Europe, one comprised of the Americas, and one stretching from Japan to Indonesia. I know not whether Australia and New Zealand or India and Pakistan would be included in an Asian trade zone. These free-trade zones would combine both technological leaders—Japan, North America, and Western Europe—with more labor-intensive countries in Southeast Asia, Central and South America, and Eastern Europe. I am admittedly biased toward the superior work force in Asia over that of the Latin American countries and Eastern Europeans.

As a result, I think double-digit unemployment will not

be uncommon in the United States. Again, higher taxes will be required to accommodate unemployed workers. Despite our status as the technological leader, the resulting jobs will not be enough to fully absorb the work force.

Transportation

Briefly, I believe public transportation—high-speed rail, subways, etc.—will grow in the United States but not at a high rate because of the expense of such projects. Air travel will grow merely because of population increases. Due to technological advances (facsimile machines, video telephones) and the incentive to reduce business costs, the need to transport persons from point A to point B will not be as great. People will resist frequent travel because of the time, inconvenience, and expense required by long-distance travel. Automobile travel, both electric and gasoline, will remain the primary mode of transportation.

Education

The need to prepare the nation's youth for the twenty-first century will require a year-round schooling, presenting another strain on the taxpayer. I believe the United States education system will be able to respond appropriately to meet the demand. I qualify this response by stating that without more support from the home, a large proportion of students will not be able to make the grade and as a result will remain economically disadvantaged throughout the remainder of their lives. Good-paying blue-collar jobs will not be available as in the past for those with no more than a high school education. As a result, they will be relegated to a lower-middle-class status for life.

Environment

Internationally, the environment will become a greater source of contention between the developed and developing nations. The Western powers and Japan in their efforts to protect the environment will attempt to restrain the burgeoning developments in the Third World areas. I think such countries will resent the heavy-handed outside interference of their richer neighbors and possibly ignore worldwide environmental restrictions. They will feel entitled to the same type of liberties with their environment as the developed countries enjoyed during their industrial eras. This would set the stage for conflict with potential cataclysmic long-term results for the planet if no worldwide agreement can be reached.

The Unthinkable Africa

Gayl Ness

With James Tobin, *The Detroit News*

Dr. Gayl D. Ness is director of the Population-Environment Dynamics Project at the University of Michigan. A sociologist, he holds positions in Michigan's departments of sociology and population planning. After studying agricultural economics at the University of Copenhagen, he acquired master's and doctoral degrees at the University of California, Berkeley. He joined Michigan's faculty in 1964, and has since written several books and scores of scholarly articles on economic development, population planning, and Southeast Asia.

If the world's population of 5.4 billion continues to grow at the current rate for only five hundred years, the planet will hold 25 trillion people, each with about 5.4 square meters of space to call his or her own.

Because this kind of growth obviously cannot continue, the future will likely see interlocking developments in three crucial fields—population control, the search for cleaner energy, and efforts to save the environment from the effects of toxification and global warming.

To understand these coming changes, we must first look backward.

For perhaps two hundred thousand years, the world's population grew exceedingly slowly. That began to change about 1700, when the growth rate rose about a tenth or a quarter of a percent per year.

Then came the invention of new machines—the steam engine, the oil well, and later the internal combustion engine—that were based on a new form of energy, fossil fuel. This allowed enormous increases in agricultural productivity and, at the same time, enormous reductions in the cost of transportation.

In the Western world, these changes produced something new—urban industrial society. With this came a much higher standard of living—more food, better nutrition and hygiene, and a decline in infectious diseases. Together, these factors substantially lowered the death rate, yet the birth rate stayed high, and thus population increased dramatically.

Then, late in the 1800s, birth rates across Europe and North America began a dramatic decline, and for an interesting reason.

In the subsistence agriculture of the old societies, children were assets; they produced a lot and took care of their parents in old age. But with the rise of modern industrial society, children become financial liabilities. If you have a child today, you pick up a bill for $150,000, and expect little or no financial return.

When Western society reached this point in the late nineteenth century, people, not surprisingly, began to limit their fertility with contraceptive technology that is as old as human beings—withdrawal and abstinence—so the birth rate and thus the growth rate dropped.

That was the story in the West. In non-Western countries, the process has been different.

After World War II, the increased productivity of the West spread to Asia, Africa, and Latin America, along with the technological breakthroughs in medicine and public health. As a result, mortality rates went down very rapidly without a drop in birth rates. Hence, population in those areas went up 3 percent annually. This was the explosion of the population bomb.

All told, the world is now growing at the rate of about 1.7 percent per year, and we simply cannot continue to grow at this rate.

First, we face a very serious threat of global warming, which is caused by the increased level in the atmosphere of "greenhouse gases," particularly carbon dioxide, which are released by burning fossil fuels. There's no question that greenhouse gases affect the world's temperature. The real question is what will happen when greenhouse gases reach much higher levels than they are now.

One great risk is the effect on temperature and precipitation. The most advanced computer model shows an increase in the global temperature of about two and a half degrees centigrade over the next one hundred years. That may bring a totally different kind of agriculture. And with seven or eight billion people, such a change may simply be too rapid for us to handle.

Take everybody's nightmare scenario, Africa, which is the real frontier in our ability to manage these changes. The population there is growing by about 3 percent per year. But agriculture has been growing by only 1 percent per year, making Africa a food-deficit region.

Now, bearing in mind the possibility of radical precipitation change, think of 1988, the recent drought year. If we had two years together like 1988, world food stocks would be almost eliminated, and there would be very little transfer of food, particularly to deficit areas. If you couldn't move food to those areas, which have high levels of debt, and there were huge food riots, what would be the capacity of those countries to repay their debts? There would be massive defaults, and the whole international monetary system could collapse.

The adjustments needed if such climate changes take place would be extremely radical. Whether we can make them is the sort of question that has scientists most concerned.

Urban industrial society, of course, has produced another set of environmental problems—chemical toxins. We live better today because of chemistry, but we don't

Come the Millennium

know what the long-term effects of that better living will be. Everywhere we look, our marvelous, affluent society has chemical time bombs build into it, and we must learn how to defuse them.

There is some good news on the population front. With the new breakthroughs in contraceptive technology, and our experience in the national family-planning programs that have spread through Asia and Latin America, we now possess the technical and organizational resolutions to some of the oldest problems in social organization.

The first challenge we face in reducing fertility is to raise the status and dignity of women. Wherever fertility has dropped, it's because women have had greater freedom to move about, become educated, and exercise their talents.

Also, wherever there are ethnic differences—blacks and whites, Malays and Chinese, Sudanese Christians and Sudanese Muslims—people are afraid to face up to the population problem because they fear their own group will decline and the opposing group will not. We have to get around that. To solve the population problem, we must build a world community that celebrates or at least accepts cultural differences.

Global warming and toxification alike require cleaner forms of technology. For that, we need research and development, and to have that, in turn, the intellectual elite in our media and universities must raise people's consciousness of the risks.

These stories—energy, population, toxification—have a great deal of human interest, and they can be told in such a way that they take a little piece of the problem and connect it to the kind of future we're leaving to our children and grandchildren.

American Society of Newspaper Editors

Ergonomics? Errrg!

If books and magazines and newspapers printed on paper are going to be museum pieces, the electronic delivery media of the future will have to address our desires for the qualities that make reading a comfortable and satisfying experience. If reading is only an option and not a necessity, it will be passed up in favor of "hotter" media unless it retains the qualities that have made it comfortable and accessible. If there are no readers, there will be no novels and poems and thoughtful essays. I don't think most people consider staring at a video screen for long periods as an attractive way to relax into a good book. Nor is scrolling through screens of text and searching through menus as appealing as spreading out the paper on the breakfast table and dripping coffee on it. All of that does not have to be lost, however, if the designers and users of the new information technology put their heads together and ponder the attributes that should be preserved. The tech people think they are doing that now, but the funny name they've tacked onto the matter—ergonomics, for gosh sakes—shows just how little we can rely on them to really get the point. Ergonomics is not an ergonomically sound word.

Parlez-Vous Español?

Sherry H. Penney

With William B. Ketter, *The Patriot Ledger*, Quincy, Mass.

> *Dr. Sherry H. Penney is chancellor of the Boston campus of the University of Massachusetts. She leads an institution that has almost twelve thousand commuter students, a faculty of more than eight hundred, and a $110 million budget. Appointed chancellor in 1988, she went to the University of Massachusetts at Boston after a fifteen-year career in educational administration at such institutions as Yale University and the State University of New York (SUNY), where she served as the system's first female vice chancellor. She is an expert on American civilization and history, with a bachelor's degree from Albion (Mich.) College, a master's from the University of Michigan, and a doctorate from SUNY.*

I hope that over the next several decades people in the United States will have gotten used to the idea of permanent change; that they will understand change is the one constant in their lives and that it should not be quite so feared as it is now.

Most notable by the year 2015 will be our much more diverse population. The rest of the country will look more like downtown Boston—a true rainbow of white, black, Hispanic, and Asian.

You will see even more of our population living in urban

areas; keep in mind that three-quarters of our population already lives in or near our cities. Unfortunately, we've been less and less willing to make our urban areas work. We are very reluctant to get away from the kind of mid-1950s idea that we're still essentially a rural nation.

We need to solve our urban problems. I worry a great deal about what's happening to the American city. I'm from the Detroit area, and I almost think that Detroit's not fixable, along with Los Angeles. Boston still is—if we get to fixing it in time. You must repair a city before it reaches a point of no return.

They've tried many things in Detroit. I know many good, smart people there, and I hope that they will be able to reverse the decline.

Now, in education, you will see more technology being used, and—because the future portends one overall educational system—there will be something of a seamless web of teaching and learning, stretching from kindergarten through college. High schools will be part of higher education, and vice versa.

Education will possess a much more international outlook. I hope—but I don't predict—that more Americans will speak an extra language. It would be very nice to say that most people early on in the next century will have another language they are fluent in besides English. The lack of a second language is one of the flaws of our society today. And it's not only speaking another language that's important here; it's what the language begins to teach you about other cultures.

Americans must understand that our way is not necessarily the right way or the best way, and if we are going to deal effectively with the rest of the world, we have to recognize—and appreciate—our differences, both abroad and at home.

If you just talk about the future of education, I believe more people will be going to college. But we will redefine the process leading to a college degree. Let me explain.

We have this magic conception ever since the twelfth century that you come to a campus, take certain subjects in college, stay for four years, and presto, you get a bachelor's degree.

But somehow we must over the next couple of decades reexamine this centuries-old process, probably advance that time table and compress the process. With such a speed up, you won't waste summers, and you won't waste Januarys. The compression could possibly create an entirely different approach to teaching and to learning.

All of our research tells us that the traditional practice of going to lectures is exactly the wrong way to learn. In fifteen years we will have awakened to the fact that the best way for people to learn—especially the more diverse population of the next century—isn't the lecture method.

Instead, a teacher will be a learner along with a group of students, rather than their lecturer. Learning will be accomplished through internship programs, hands-on work, immediate feedback, computers—these will be the keys to success.

Such new ways of teaching and learning will have to be accomplished without infusions of new money from state and federal governments. There will be fewer tax dollars for education primarily because Americans won't want to pay additional taxes for it anymore.

The education bill will have to be paid by parents and students, and that is a big social policy change. What it signals is that society says education is not necessarily a public good to be supported by public funds, but an individual responsibility.

I predict such a change, but I hope it doesn't happen. I only predict it because of what already is going on throughout the United States. More than 65 percent of the states last year cut budgets for all of their state higher-education institutions. The cuts have been snowballing over the last four or five years, and the trend is bound to continue.

Students of the future will be older. They will have to pay more of the bill so they will work, then go to college, or work part-time and go to school part-time.

On my campus, for instance, the average student age today is twenty-seven. The graduate student age is something like thirty-five or thirty-six. We have many people on their own and that number will grow. The result: More people will be going to college in their thirties and forties and even fifties. Our university granted a bachelor's degree a year ago to a woman who had twelve children and twelve grandchildren.

In tomorrow's new world of higher education we'll have more interdisciplinary research and more interdisciplinary teaching, creating a better, more responsive learning climate for students. Call what I've just described cluster education, cooperative education, or call it collaborative learning.

All of us got a general education by majoring in history or whatever, and taking some English and perhaps other courses on the side. Very few of us had an integrated educational experience, one that forced us to realize that on the job and in life you use all of what you've learned every minute of the day.

Nowadays, students take a history course and a test. They close that book and go to another course. English, history and math are all connected—part of a holistic knowledge and skill base—and you really can't function without a little or a lot of all of these disciplines.

I tell people who can't buy this concept that when I go to my job, I don't practice English from nine to ten, math from ten to eleven, and my history skills from eleven to twelve. I have to blend all those things every minute of the day. Yet there's nothing in anybody's educational experience to help them do that kind of blending of knowledge and skill.

The other thing that's going to change is the school year. We're definitely moving toward the year-round school year. Students won't take the summer off. I promise you we will have a terrible time getting used to this idea, but what we do today is inefficient.

I think it is crazy, when you look around the country, to see so many schools—both K–12 and higher education—shut down during the summer. That's a wasteful use of both people and resources.

I foresee technology playing a much larger role in higher education. I would hope that every student who graduates from UMass Boston is computer literate. We need to bring technology to bear on learning and teaching.

The computer will permit us to be able to do more academically off campus. You won't have to come to a campus like ours three days a week. Maybe you'd only have to come here twice a month. However, you would still learn.

With the computer you can give students an exercise and they can do it at home or during their lunch hour at work. The computer will give them instant response. With such technology, you might learn in two days what now takes five. Computers will serve as tutors, as adjuncts to the faculty.

No, I don't think professors will be eliminated, but what we will see is an appropriate marriage of machines and people, both in and out of the lecture hall, seminar room, and laboratory.

Technology will change the way we do our teaching because it will free us up from some of the rigid classroom practices we now use.

There is another trend—the invasion of the workplace by the university. There's going to be a bigger demand to bring education to where people are. Many people find it difficult to both hold a job and then, amid family demands, trek to the campus to attend a late-afternoon or evening course.

One idea I've been gnawing on for the last several years is the need for all of us in education to develop a sense of leadership among our students. We must determine what kind of leadership and leaders we need, and then determine how to develop leadership and leaders.

Right now we don't have a clue how to train leaders, and we seem also to have lost the ability to some degree to train citizens in citizenship. My colleagues and I worry about this. We worry about it every time the community tries to elect someone to public office.

What worries me is that anybody who takes the risk to

be a leader—and I'll use President Clinton as an example—is heatedly criticized and dumped on for her or his mistakes. That sort of atmosphere makes anybody who might want to be a public official to say, "Do I really want to do that?"

If you're looking out several decades from now, one of the questions you ought to examine is, "Who are the leaders going to be, and where are they going to come from?" Well, I don't have the answer.

Will there be a woman president within the next fifteen years? I sure hope so, though I would predict not. Maybe vice president. It is more possible we will have an African American president before we have a woman president. First, however, we will have a vice president of color.

There are still so few women who hold the top administrative positions in higher education. The latest figures (1989) show that there are only slightly over three women chief executive officers of U.S. colleges and universities. That's about 10 percent of the total cohort. Of course, that percentage will rise, but now there certainly is an imbalance, particularly when you consider that the majority of all students in higher education are female.

Religion will play a greater role in the year 2015 than it did in the past fifteen years when we seem to have rejected it. In the future it will take form that won't seem disconnected from life. When my kids rejected religion it was because it seemed disconnected to anything that mattered to them.

Religion has to find more relevance to what is happening in society. I've been fascinated by some of the things that the black church has been doing recently with social action activities.

I think you'll see more of that, because as our population gets grayer and grayer, and lonelier and lonelier, it will need something to hold on to, and religion can meet a need.

People will still be reading newspapers fifteen years from now, but your competition will be the many other sources from which people get news. People will get live news—in color and motion—on airplanes, on the subway, in their cars, you name it. Indeed, some of the methods of delivering news will be interactive. That's your challenge and your opportunity.

A Diploma in Degrees

Lowell Catlett

With Tim Gallagher, *Albuquerque Tribune*

Prof. Lowell Catlett teaches and conducts research in the areas of marketing, policy, futures markets, management, and futuristic issues in the Agricultural Economics and Business Department at New Mexico State University. His Ph.D. in economics is from Iowa State University. He is co-author of a textbook and two books being published in 1994 and has received numerous teaching awards, including being voted Teacher of the Year at New Mexico State.

There's a major transformation going on in the workplace. One-third of the labor force works wherever they want to. In the next twenty years, close to 85 percent will work when and where they want to. New jobs essentially will come to the people. The workplace is defined by what the worker wants it to be.

The changes in where people will work will mean phenomenal adjustments in the major cities. Fringe cities will pop up close to present center cities, but will not have the problems of today's urban communities. People will move wherever they want. Cities will still be around, but people will be living less in suburban areas and more in rural areas.

Work

The authoritarian mode is dying and being replaced by clusters, teams, flat management. There's an emphasis on interplay among people. When you have people working where they want, you don't have someone giving orders. You have groups of people getting things done. It's very quickly obvious who knows how to get it done and who doesn't. It's not through credentials that people will get ahead, it'll be through what they can do.

Education

So it'll be no longer important to get a bachelor's degree. The question being asked will be, "Can you function in a team and get things done?" Our generation had to hack away to become proficient at computers. But computer-science people only care about "Can you do it? Can you get it done?"

Technology is driving all of the changes in education. Time, place, and form are important. The University of Phoenix branch in Albuquerque draws tremendous numbers of students, because it offers a variety of courses at night and on weekends. People are opting for what they want. In the new world of teams, does it matter whether the degree is from Harvard? What matters to the person getting the degree is "Where can I get the education?" Education takes on the form of work training. You will see this falling back into the high school level. You won't need a diploma. You will need a certificate saying you have achieved certain levels of competency. Then the barriers will come down. But, here's a caution. This won't happen quickly. Generations will have to pass before people will give up the old ways of doing things.

Making Lines

Now we have a demarcation. Here's life, here's school, here's work. What matters is time, choice, and "Do you know it?" My life is now my choice for leisure, life, work, and education. My life is choice, convenience, and time. What's education and what's work will become a big blur. You already are seeing changes in culture.

Entertainment

Because of virtual reality, we no longer have passive entertainment. But this generation wants interactive entertainment. The next big growth area is experiences. Take the wine country, for example. Now, they will let you stay there and help crush grapes on your vacation. People want an experience. I don't want to be a newspaper editor, but I would like to know what it's like. The learning that goes on is incredible.

Because of this integration of work and leisure, I see no retirement.

Agriculture

Computer-based technology is changing what we do about agriculture. The Douglas fir tree communicates through alo-chemicals. Through smell. They emit alo-chemicals. They say to themselves, "I'm infected with a beetle. So I've got to protect myself." They will take chemical action to protect themselves.

In the future, we will have a pesticide that emits the opposite pattern so the insect is not attracted to the plant. (Mercedes-Benz is designing a no-muffler car because it will have sound waves on the opposite wave pattern that negate the noise waves.) No chemical application. It is the philosophy of understanding that plants and animals communicate with each other in an ecosystem.

Bio-tech is coming into its own. Remember this word, "Foodaceuticals." How do we manage that tomato? With a flavor-saver. We take the "rot" gene out so that the tomato won't rot for weeks or months and we don't even have to refrigerate it. We've already made those plants more beneficial to you in nutrients. Now we're moving to new levels of managing nutrition.

Come the Millennium

The food system will be even safer. We're feeding the world better. We are producing 2,700 calories of food for people a day. That's up from 2,000 calories a day in 1960. The blur comes in with industrial products and drugs. They are engineering bacteria to eat solid wastes. Fifty percent of the waste in this country could be eaten by this bacteria and it creates ethanol. We'd be cleaning up waste and creating energy. Want to know why large companies are so interested in protecting the rain forest? Because most of the pharmaceuticals come from the world's plants and animals. You separate things so you can understand them better, but in the end they all work together.

We are finally getting sophisticated enough to understand in the ecosystem that the whole is bigger than the sum of the parts.

American Society of Newspaper Editors

Something to Choke On
Most people read their newspapers over breakfast now, so why not combine the two? Churchy La Femme, the philosopher-poet turtle in Pogo, once proposed a novel solution to uncertain economic times. Print money on edible things, like cheese slices. The rationale was that as long as you had money, you'd never have to starve. Edible newspapers would take care of the recycling problem in the bargain.

Feminization of Dux

Michele Deasy

With Judy Brown,
The Herald, New Britain, Conn.

Michele Deasy is a director of the New Britain, Conn., Youth Museum. A classical scholar, as is her husband Dr. John Schmaker, president of Central Connecticut State University, she holds a master's degree in classics from Ohio State University and a bachelor's degree from the University of California at Irvine. She previously was assistant dean of undergraduate studies at the State University of New York (SUNY) at Albany.

The mother of two young sons, she is a member of the National Association of Women Deans, the American Philological Association, the Classical Association of the Atlantic States, and the Rotary Club of New Britain.

As a classics scholar and mother of two boys, I feel strongly that the family is here to stay, configured in different ways for different times.

Most people have good values. They just aren't making news; they're busy making dinner. You don't do drama out of ordinary lives, and the need for it is fulfilled, to a certain extent, by newspapers. Certainly there are serious problems in our society and difficult times. We all need an oasis somewhere to allow ourselves to grow. We are and can be living together fairly well, with memories that go back for centuries.

In a recent speech to the local YWCA luncheon, I pointed out that Livy, writing about Dido, the Queen of Carthage, noted in amazement that *Dux femina:* "a woman was leader." The word leader is masculine, and no feminine form of it exists. I believe that in the future it will be in the plural and commonplace for women. Women will be the leaders.

I am optimistic about the environment and feel that it is not a fringe concern anymore, but is the responsibility of everyone and particularly schoolchildren. We have a vice president who is an environmental specialist, and every child is aware of recycling and our dependence upon a healthy environment. Europeans may think we are crazy, but America has come around.

We can, however, take a lesson from Europeans, with transportation where Americans have been very short-sighted. There is no excuse for us not to have clean, convenient, on-time land transportation. We have jet engines, why not speedy trains?

Actually, I firmly believe that nothing can replace newspapers. You can read them when and where you want and newspaper readers are less hassled than TV watchers. There will always be a place for the locally oriented newspaper, which tells what is happening in the community. Speaking specifically of *The Herald,* I like its up-news or "good stuff."

As time goes by, rigid people will lose out. You have to keep your options open, and with every job you have, learn something extra. My advice to young people is to major in something you love. Women have come a long way, but lack the time to keep up friendships, or the solitude to keep a journal and to correspond with friends. When women are working full-time, with children at home, the nonprofessional relationships and friendships suffer. There will, thus, be no record for future generations as to how things were, as telephone calls just aren't the same.

Among the good things that have happened in our society are the popularization of art and the education system. Every society has its popular customs, and ours is dominated by TV appealing to generally low-brow tastes. If people choose, TV will do the talking and this is dangerous. As for children and TV, we can always turn it off. With today's economy, however, I think more families will be interested in taking day trips to historic locations and to parks, and this is a good thing. The family unit, which has certainly survived through the centuries, is a truth of the past and a forecast for the future in which I firmly believe.

Managing Oxymorons

Jagdish Sheth

With Ron Martin,
Atlanta Journal and Constitution

Rated as one of the top ten marketing professors in the country, Jagdish Sheth is also a fellow of the American Psychology Association. His books include the classic The Theory of Buyer Behavior *with John A. Howard. He has worked as a consultant and seminar leader for major corporations in the United States, Europe, and Asia. Born in Burma, he came to the United States as a student in the 1960s. Dr. Sheth previously taught at the University of Southern California for seven years, the University of Illinois for fifteen years, Columbia University for five years, and MIT for two years.*

Q: We're talking about fifteen to twenty-five years from today. One thing I'm really curious about is that we know that folks in the last twenty years have been working more, have less leisure time, become much more stressed. Talk a little bit about whether you think that's going to continue.
A: Maybe I'll set the stage by summarizing the two major trends and what they are changing.

One is that the demographics of the people are getting much more divergent . . . [in] four areas:

1. The aging of the population. Life expectancy has gone up from forty-nine years in the early 1900s and it is only about eighty years right now. That is extending further out. The fastest-growing segment is of people who live to be one hundred years or older. By the year 2030, we will have four million living people one hundred years or older. The second fastest growing segment is eighty or older. The American Association of Retired Persons is becoming the most powerful political membership organization.

2. Multigenerational families. Four generations will be living together in one household. That's never happened before. The four are the pre-World War I generation, the generation born between World War I and 1946, the baby boomers (those born between 1946 and 1964), and the fourth is the generation born after 1964. In at least twenty metropolitan areas, college-educated single wage earners cannot afford housing.

3. Life-style. There is no one single life-style. The typical family where the husband is the breadwinner and the wife is the homemaker taking care of the children is now down to 7 percent of the U.S. population. The majority of adult women over eighteen are now working outside of the family. These working-women households will increase to 65 percent of the population by the year 2000.

4. Income. The next generation cannot sustain current standards of living on a single-wage income. They will need a dual income by and large.

Each one of these trends has tremendous impacts on the way we behave in the workplace and the way we make decisions in the marketplace.

For example, to get back to the aging, when I grow older my needs will shift altogether. My biggest concern is health care. Therefore, health care has been taking a larger and larger share of the gross national product. By the year 2000, it will be 15.3 percent of GNP, or about $1.3 trillion to $1.4 trillion.

And I tend to become health conscious as I grow older. I begin to read the packages before I put the contents in my mouth. I get into physical fitness. All of a sudden walking becomes the biggest active recreation for people. Golf becomes popular. These are the lower-impact sports.

In the workplace, you are very conscious of health and want a smoke-free environment and are concerned by the employer's health-benefits package

Q: Is there an awareness of impending violence between the generations? Is the feeling among the older generation one of "I earned this money. It's mine to spend"?

A: The older generation is also the most affluent generation in America today. Since the present generation is now the poorest, imagine what happens when they all live under one roof. Class conflict is going to become generational, and can happen within families. People from the younger generation are telling their parents and grandparents, "You can't keep all that money." At one time we thought government would be the one that would balance income differences, for taxation and entitlement. You tax the rich and give entitlements to the poor. Now income distribution is sharper within a family. There will be much more debate and discussion and, unfortunately, since we have access to guns so much in this country, we're going to see trigger-happy people. We will see more and more adult children killing their parents to get access to the money.

Q: Given this, which generation is likely to resort to revolution?

A: I think the last post-1964 generation probably is the one, somebody born in the seventies or eighties and is just about to become an adult. They're going to start rebelling.

Q: What about the workplace?

A: We have to have more flexibility. The old stereotypes in the workplace have to go away. More and more women will be joining the work force. You will see more issues such as sexual harassment.

I think the workplace was never organized for an equal number of women working at the office or factory. Bathrooms and other physical facilities are not organized for women. Chairs, desks, etc., were organized for men, not women. There will be more safety and security issues that will come up.

And especially among white-collar workers, more and more women will say that they do not want to work sixty or sixty-five hours a week, that they have a family to manage and will work part time for twenty or twenty-five hours a week. There will be more job sharing, with two people using the same desk or office—one in the morning and the other in the afternoon. Flexible work hours is what employers will have to learn how to authorize.

And because we will have a majority of women working, companies will have to rework nepotism policies that prevent husbands and wives from working in the same firm. In fact, smart companies are saying, "If these are two career-oriented people, both are excellent, why not move them together?" So career planning is very different now.

Q: What about the media?

A: The aging of the population, the divergence of lifestyles, and the impact of new technology are already affecting the media. A newspaper cannot do what the telephone can do. The telephone cannot do what cameras can do. Cameras cannot do what the television can do. Today, with digital technology, we are heading into interactive media.

And since there will no longer be a single dominant life-style, there is no such thing as a single newspaper that can satisfy everybody. How many magazines do we have today? Forty-five thousand? The cost of producing one is minimal with desktop publishing. I can target a niche and produce a magazine to cater to that group. There will be more and more specialized newspapers coming out. The general-purpose newspaper is not going to be the future.

And look at radio and TV. When I am older, I'm more interested in adult reality than in fantasy. I am very interested in "60 Minutes" because that's the real world out there. Talk shows are becoming more popular because they're based on reality. Twenty-four-hour news is now big business. ABC has abandoned the whole rock 'n' roll format on their radio stations, most of which are now 24-hour talk show formats.

Newspapers have been very traditional and have not kept up with these changes.

As you know, the daily papers especially, not all print media, but daily newspapers have been shrinking with the advent of twenty-four-hour news, both in radio as well as broadcast media. In most major cities, therefore, there is only one major newspaper. Consolidation has taken place and even the government has allowed mergers and acquisitions within a given market, even though it may constitute monopolizing.

Print media, however, will still continue to grow but will take a different form. What was a general-purpose print medium is going to become more and more specialized for specialized activities. Print media will come back again. I have a very interesting discovery. I find that anything that was general-purpose or anything that was a mainstream activity but was given up by society, it always comes back either as a hobby or as a specialization: hunting, fishing, gardening, baking breads, cooking. Same thing will happen with the media.

The real large-scale national newspapers will do well. *Wall Street Journal, New York Times,* maybe *Los Angeles Times, Investors Daily,* those kinds of papers, will have no problem because they are specialized in their focus and their market is national. The newspapers that will have problems are those dealing primarily with local events, relying on local retail advertising, and local classified advertising.

That's where the biggest change is taking place. We're talking of cable being able to create a five-hundred-channel capability at a local level. The key point is that it's not a national event, it's really a city-by-city event. At a local level in each city, if you offer a local channel what you are doing is shifting the advertising revenue from the local retailers, such as grocery stores, department stores, and local classified ads onto the cable channel.

The economics are very powerful. It is cheaper to advertise on cable than in print media. It is more timely because you can do it on an ongoing basis. For example, take classified ads. Classified ads require no creative work, no artwork, no setup, no logos, but maybe a number of people

Come the Millennium

call in to say they want to place a classified ad. Immediately, as the classified-ad recipient person keys in the information, it can appear on the screen on local TV.

And they can do more creative work. In addition, they can be more creative if they want to include video and graphics. And this will be on the air twenty-four hours, updated constantly.

Q: That's already happening. There is a local channel which advertises homes for sale and things like that.

A: Yes, but this one will be massive because it will be a channel that virtually duplicates what a newspaper classified section does: homes for sale, employment, cars. In addition, it can also have other information that a newspaper currently provides.

Q: In other words, we're talking about a channel, any station today which would provide news, sports, classified. Everything a newspaper does.

A: Absolutely. Imagine, with today's technology even, you can have something about sports and then an editorial about auto racing and ads by sports companies. There can be ads with a degree of customization. More important is the local grocery store and a local department store, such as Rich's, which are the main advertising sources of revenue for newspapers today, could lease a channel. They don't even have to work with a local TV station. With the powerful but cheap technology available, they can do in-house productions about their services and products and advertise them on these channels. They won't need to spend money advertising in newspapers anymore.

I believe when that happens, newspapers in cities with populations of between one hundred thousand to five hundred thousand won't be able to sustain their revenue and will have to close. In the bigger cities, New York, Los Angeles, or even Atlanta, the base is big enough to have several advertising outlets, but even in these cities, you may end up having just one paper a city.

But these newspapers, too, will have to move toward mass customization. That's a contradiction in terms but the future is all about managing oxymorons. What mass

81

customization says is that the production is standard but the product is of tremendous variety.

The standard content is packaged into as many specialized markets as possible. What we do now is come out with a newspaper with sections inside: Lifestyles, Sports, Business, Community. What I'm saying is you need another format that is quickly efficient so that you could customize it down to even ZIP code level. The news is the same but it is packaged differently, depending on the area it serves. Free weeklies do that. If you can do that then I think those are the future formats for newspapers.

Q: Let's take a practical example, the *Atlanta Constitution.* You would have one for the city and one for Gwinnett.

A: Exactly.

Q: The same news except you take the Gwinnett news and put it on the front page and the other sections have the Gwinnett stuff highlighted.

A: Exactly.

Q: So instead of having a separate Gwinnett Extra, you would have the whole paper as Gwinnett, with the contents the same, just repackaged?

A: Right.

Q: What about readers? Everybody says that newspapers are losing readers. The aging of America seems to indicate that people read more as they grow older.

A: I personally think that the readership of print media is something that will never die. Actually it's going to come back again in a bigger way. It's always been one phenomenon taking mass dominance, and then a reaction setting in. So I think the next generation of young people will be reading more. But I think what newspapers have to do is go back to a different content, which is where the readership is.

Newspapers believe very strongly in offering what is timely, what is immediate, but they cannot compete against other media more visual on this basis. With a camera out there, you see a live scene on TV of fighting in Kuwait. There's no way newspapers can do that.

Newspapers need to become daily encyclopedias. People want information. They don't want news from newspapers, but information such as information about health. It is not news as you think of news. Primarily it will be like a daily encyclopedia, with lots of useful information, but also providing perspective.

Q: So, you think newspapers should move away from hard news toward backgrounders, commentary, opinions?

A: Exactly, opinions. More and more columnists and experts writing on a daily basis. More and more information such as advice columns. Things that people want to know more about but can't get from radio or TV. Listening is not sufficient to get all the information I want. I want to be able to read more and save the item. That's how people store books. They store magazines they really want to read at their leisure several times.

Q: Does it mean that we have to get away from the idea of newspapers being a product with a twenty-four-hour shelf life?

A: Exactly. Newspapers have so much capability they don't exploit for commercial purposes. Journalists are trained to be almost anti-business, but more and more, journalism and business are becoming closer. The information you collect has a huge resale value. Just like TV and its reruns, newspapers must learn how to commercialize the information they collect and be able to reuse it again and again. News is perishable, but information is not.

Q: What should papers do to target readers and attract market segments, such as women readers?

A: Readership is growing but papers are not capturing their share of this growing readership. Children's magazines are growing, women's magazines are growing. Women used to be the main readers of newspapers, but the number of women working will increase to 65 percent. A woman also takes care of the family, so she does not have the discretionary time she used to have. So, morning delivery means nothing to her.

The only little discretionary time she has is when she comes home in the evening. That is her time. How do you get into that time, competing with magazines and TV?

American Society of Newspaper Editors

You have to capture her share of mind and time for information.

If you can organize that, think of a newspaper as serving not a whole family but a paper that serves a father, a mother, a teenager. You could have three newspapers, why not, instead of one mass paper? We have four TV sets, six radios, two cars in a house —why not have three papers?

And cost is not a problem. The backup office has become very efficient now with digitalization. We can do this mass customization. I think the biggest cost is going to be the print run. But as we go more and more toward desktop publishing and digital information collection, that cost should come down.

Let's say everyone has a PC, there's no need for printing at all. People can have the information delivered electronically and print out on their own printers what aspect of this information they want. In the short run, you have to improvise and say you won't have only one paper in the house but maybe two—you could have a general paper and perhaps another paper only for women.

The price must be affordable. After all, the woman will say I can hear a radio free and watch TV for free, so why should I pay for this extra information? That's the part where she makes the trade-off to say that the information is so valuable I can't do without it. It contains information that can help me with my job, my life, my family.

That's why if a newspaper becomes more and more an information service as opposed to news and entertainment, gets away from that and toward information and education, I think that will work. The concept of the encyclopedia rather than a news media.

Q: Should we abandon news to the broadcast media, then?
A: Two options. One is to say you will do the gathering because you have the expertise to do that but you would not publish the paper. You would become collectors of information but not distributors of information. The broadcast media would do that.

To me, broadcast and print media are complementary.

After all, the broadcast media take their cues from the print media. They read the *New York Times* and the *Wall Street Journal* and the local paper and pick up stuff. Local radio stations pick up topics from the paper and use them as subject on talk shows.

Your have the capability to separate the two functions of collecting information and distributing it. That's possible. Perhaps, you don't need a daily newspaper. Maybe you could even have a biweekly format.

Or, by using mass customization, you can have a newspaper for specific areas. You can come out with a paper, say, an *Atlanta Constitution* for the city, a *Gwinnett Constitution* for Gwinnett and a *Macon Constitution*. Each are their own little papers. *L.A. Times* is already doing this. They are in an area that is the seventh largest economy in the world and they say we will serve that economy. So, they're customizing papers for areas north, east, and south of LA.

You have a centralized information-collection office and then printing and distribution plants around the state, say. You can even have a collection plant in the U.S. and have printing and distribution plants around the world to which you send the information electronically and produce customized papers for each specific area or region or nation. It is done by *Wall Street Journal* and *USA Today*. It can be done by others.

Q: The topics people are interested in are?
A: Legal matters, health and medicine, food, physical fitness, fashion, science, technology, sports. As we are inundated by information, people want someone to comment on it. They want someone to say what all this means for them. That is where columnists come in. You get well-known columnists or experts to comment.

Newspapers should explain what is happening instead of merely reporting it. Newspapers, as they got more competition from broadcast media, delegated national and global news to that media and concentrated on local news because local TV news did not do the job. But now, local TV has caught up. So my view is that it is not news at all that is going to be the future, but information.

And the two media are complementary. Once I see or hear about something on TV or radio, I want to learn more about it. I want someone to explain it and put it in perspective. So I turn to my newspaper, just as broadcast media read newspapers and use topics highlighted in papers for their on-air shows.

Every time newspapers do an investigative report about some phenomenon puzzling the community they do very well. For example, the Tokars case in Atlanta. But it doesn't have to be local. Newspapers can do a better job explaining what's happening in Bosnia, for example, than TV. They can provide the historical background and the perspective. It's the sort of thing people clip and save. It is information.

Q: Is mass media dead?

A: Mass media is dead because there is no mass market anymore. Now we have a niche consumption society, not a mass consumption society. From broadcast to narrowcast to monocast—you have to customize to the segment of one.

Q: Where do you see multimedia going in the home of the future?

A: The home will have two separate integrated devices. One will be primarily for recreation. That will be the evolution of the current TV set into a multimedia station. The screen will be the dominant point, but remote will have a microphone, it will be able to work as a cordless phone and even as a video phone.

The TV set will then have all capabilities such as graphics, motion, text. It will be my gateway to the outside world for entertainment, shopping, and other transactions and information, maybe education. It will also be a video-audio set. It will be here at the turn of the century for under $1,000.

The second device will be centered on the personal computer, which will be for business purposes. The screen won't be that important, but it will also be multimedia and the storage will be in CD-ROM. It will be my own personal device, with massive memory and processing capabilities. It will be used more for my business.

Come the Millennium

In Your Own World
Get used to it. Nothing can be preserved exactly as it always has been, no matter how well it worked in its time. Newspapers have managed to reflect that over the last couple of centuries. This is no time to want to stop. There are looming opportunities to reach and inform segments of the potential recipients that certainly don't seem to be reading newspapers today. Because households may have every conceivable kind of software, one of the most intriguing possibilities of all is allowing the recipients to customize what and how they receive from their end. Every "newspaper" could be a unique item, with information selected and presented in a form suited to the individual reader.

Invest in Coffee Shops

Winslow Wedin

With John Christie, Fort Lauderdale Sun-Sentinel

Winslow Wedin is an architect and urban planner in Boca Raton, Fla. He has degrees in architecture, urban planning, and systems analysis and has been in private practice since 1959. He is the founder of the Palm Beach Futures Group, which is associated with the World Futures Society.

In 1982, I came up with a project for myself: to develop a city of the future. All architects dream of doing whole cities. I envisioned two distinct worlds. One is the enclosed, extremely private type home, where TV and the various media—computers, CD-ROM and all these—will be enough for a person to get worldwide information, entertainment, sports. But then there is also a real need for social interaction. I used as my model EPCOT. You have the grand esplanade around the lake and all the pavilions around that, and I envision the little pavilions being theaters, concert halls, coffee shops, arcades, spiritual centers, whatever—a total social, personal interaction. The same with shopping. I predicted the home shopping network, knowing that it was on the horizon. Why have to go shopping for Peter Pan peanut butter? We know it by the jar. We can select that on television and have it delivered to our home with all the name brands. The only thing we would want to pick on a personal level are perishables, fruits, vegetables, that need to be looked at, smelled, etc. So the truck farms would come back into the core.

My vision of the city of the future would be a combination of very remote sorts of things—computer-oriented, television-oriented—and very, very much a kind of shaking-hands coffee shop.

Talking very locally, we have an opportunity here in Boca to do exactly what I was conceptually thinking of with Mizner Park (an existing outdoor shopping district) by having Boca Museum, the Caldwell Theater, the Children's Museum there—a social gathering place with all the specialty shops that did get there and coffee shops and restaurants that did get there. It happened at a commercial level, rather than a social level.

Getting back to habitat, what's out is suburban living and what's in is small towns. Big cities are going to have to be evacuated. People can't take the crime, the congestion, traffic problems, etc., all its cultural advantages notwithstanding. Little towns are giving quality of life-style: walk to school, walk to shop, don't worry about locking your door.

We will have an extended age with the health benefits and quality of life improving. We may reach 100, 120, and still be productive. There's going to be a greater proportion of senior citizens alive and able to do their jobs.

Regarding information needs, we're talking a total information system not limited to computer media, TV, radio, media, or newspapers—the whole thing becomes possibly a network of information: local, current, long-range, whatever. But I'm going to give you an example of something that is cutting edge that maybe doesn't work. I belong to a number of national architectural newsletter groups. One had a little newsletter that came out using Xerox reproduction. They decided to update it and they jumped into videocassettes. We get five or six cassettes every year. This is fantastic: You get a sense of three dimension, walking through the building, seeing the scale, with people moving through it that you can't get from a photograph. Except, the problem is that when the videocassette comes in, you put it in the machine, you watch it. You may watch it a second time. Some is good, some is bad. You fast-forward, you reverse. You relook over something that is of interest you two, three, times and you put it on the shelf. The opportunity to go get the video and put it in the machine again is very slight. How many times do you ever re-view a movie you bought? Once, maybe. But a magazine, a book, a newspaper—something of that type you say, "Oh, there was something on page 57 I wanted to show you," and you open it up. The hand-held media I think are still extremely valuable. Computer drafting and drawing—it's marvelous on the screen, but there's something about putting it down on a piece of paper and taking a redline pencil and marking it up and thinking about it while you're marking it up that is, at least I find, very valuable. Printed matter gives you random access.

I tend to be very interested in low-cost housing. I'm working with developers and entrepreneurs on a ten- to fifteen-thousand-dollar house. Small, efficient, made of recycled materials. Grandmother's cottages. I think our zoning should allow another unit on the back of our properties for such things. But that has to do with government. I think they have much more control than they should. Codes and regulations, among my professional associates, these things come up all the time. They do not trust the professionals—architects, engineers—to do their job. They're saying no, no, no. If you're talking adding fifteen thousand dollars for code regulations, you can't build a fifteen-thousand-dollar house.

The future is a very short thing. It creeps up on us. To look ahead forty years is important, but extremely difficult.

Come the Millennium

Step Aside, Flash Gordon
The safest thing that can be said about the future is that it will not very likely be what we expect. Now that I am old enough to have gone from a past into some of the future, one of my main disappointments is that architecture has not turned out the way we were promised by the pulp science-fiction magazines, Flash Gordon serials, and the 1939 World's Fair. I was really counting on the soaring delicate spires and the highways in the sky ribboning around them, and everybody having personal hover-vehicles. That stuff hasn't come to pass, but on the other hand, I live and work in a house with two VCRs, a copier, and a fax machine, none of which Flash Gordon ever had.

Mr. and Mrs. Village

Patricia B. Cronin

With Dan Warner,
The Lawrence (Mass.) *Eagle-Tribune*

Dr. Patricia B. Cronin is a psychologist and associate professor of psychology at Bradford College, a small liberal arts college in Massachusetts. Holder of the Abby Milton O'Neil Distinguished Professorship, an endowed chair, she spends almost as much time off campus in a variety of community activities. She received her bachelor of arts degree in sociology and anthropology from the University of California at Santa Barbara, where she was Phi Beta Kappa, and her masters and doctorate in psychology from Kansas State University.

Every day, more than 2,200 American children drop out of school.

Every day, 3,610 American teenagers are assaulted, 630 are robbed. and 80 are raped.

Every day, thirteen Americans age fifteen to twenty-four commit suicide and another sixteen are murdered.

Every day, five hundred adolescents begin using illegal drugs and one thousand begin drinking alcohol.

Every day, one thousand unwed teenage girls become mothers.

Every day, one hundred thousand high school students bring guns to school.

And I have just finished reading a recent copy of *News-*

week. The first story as I turned inside is headed "Life Means Nothing." It is about a Houston teenage gang that killed two girls by standing on their necks, but even the manner of death isn't what shocked the community. What shocked was the gangs' lack of any visible remorse. "We hit the big time," was a gang member's response when told he would be charged with murder. The middle-spread feature was on the rising tide of violence on the job. And the cover story told of an America seeking new and bigger thrills. The issue of *Newsweek* is nothing unusual; typical fare, a week of news. I do not know where we will be a decade from now, but it is clear where we are headed: for trouble.

I am afraid for a large segment of our society and for the family. We are raising a battered and burned out generation; one where violence is commonplace as children endeavor to simply grow up. It permeates their entertainment, their school day, their perambulation through the neighborhood, their newspapers, their six o'clock TV news, and, all too often, their family lives.

Children and their parents seem to have lost a sense of control over their own destinies. Whether or not it is true that they have lost control is irrelevant, what is important is that they think and feel that they have lost control. Violence is increasingly viewed as a solution for the frustrations of life.

While there is no direct psychological link between frustration and aggression, we Americans seem all too often to turn to one form or another of aggression when frustrated. The violence often accompanies a lack of hope. Young people say they are violent because they see no hope for the future. Parents see a lack of control everywhere. An example: What parent among you thinks you have any control whatsoever over what your children are exposed to in terms of violence and language? I shielded my son from certain TV shows, then sent him to kindergarten. In the space of one recess—what's that, twenty minutes?—he had down pat the whole plots of the tube's most popular and violent cartoon shows. And because violence is everywhere—and because it is so prevalent and so glorified in the media—the desensitization factor is high. People adapt to conditions as a matter of psychological survival. We adapt by becoming increasingly less shocked and disturbed by violence. That adaptation gives us a survival edge, but it can also be our worst enemy. It makes violence commonplace; a part of life. It allows the violence to grow as a part of our culture.

There is little general respect for teachers, the police, or adults. Kids often disregard and disrespect our institutions—the courts, the law, schools, churches, what have you. Thus, many have lost a sense of stability and structure. The neighborhoods they are growing up in are all too frequently destabilized because they are undergoing rapid population changes. Parents and adults in destabilized neighborhoods don't seem to transmit positive norms and values. Kids give up—they don't have hope for themselves and their lives.

And kids are picking up this disrespect from adults and the world we've created for them; one generation is teaching the other a lack of basic civility.

I am not saying that we are a society becoming unglued like ancient Rome. But we are on a waxed, slippery slope downward toward being unglued. I don't think we have hit bottom. I hope we don't have to before getting our wake-up call.

So what will the next decade be about?

It will be about how families negotiate life.

They need help.

The help they need is not as simple as providing day care and elder care and economic opportunities or even in fixing our schools, as important as all those things are. We need to rethink the role of families and children in society. We don't value either enough.

There is an old African phrase: "It takes a village to raise a child." Changing things means mobilizing the entire community. We need to care more and put money where our mouth is. This means schools must do business differently and business must restructure the way it approaches families and children. Both need to give children and parents a reason to get up in the morning, to have hope. Business needs to become involved in education; to provide mentors for kids coming up. We need to build coalitions of businesses, schools, parents, and more. This is a complicated society. We need to coalesce all elements to find solutions.

But, mostly, we need to get back to basics; to restore a sense of civility and hope to our world. The psychological research shows that basic values—a structure where people exchange respect for one another, a safe and supportive family and neighborhood, an environment where students are allowed to express themselves regardless of their capability, a set of expectations that looks toward success and a family atmosphere free of conflict—are what make a better family and a better society. The actual family structure—one or two parents—isn't as important as the way the family carries on its day-to-day interaction.

This is basic stuff. It may seem simple, but it is not as simple as "Father Knows Best." The world is different now than it was when I grew up. We must honor diversity, worry about gender bias, and understand different family structures, but there still can be a common sense of discourse that leads to respectful interactions.

We will not have the warm, fuzzy sense of the 1940s, but we can do a little bit better.

And newspapers can help.

Some thoughts on how.

EMPHASIZE THE CONSEQUENCES of violent acts. Right now, I see too much of simple reporting on violence in a manner that tends to glorify; that adds to the desensitization effect. Our troubled kids cry for attention. They don't care whether attention is negative, for at least negative attention is better than no attention at all. There is a case in a neighboring town where a boy bashed a girl in the head with a baseball bat, killing her. Day after day of testimony was reported. Buried deep inside one story was a paragraph that he is a very miserable young man right now. Kids need to see those consequences clearly. It may mean more follow up stories to make clear the misery that violence causes not only to others but especially to the perpetrator. We need to become more responsible for our actions and their consequences.

SET A TONE OF CIVILITY for the world in how you write. Try courtesy titles, Mr., Mrs., Miss, Ms. Use respectful language as you write. Be sure that all races, creeds, and colors are shown the same sense of respect. Better to leave out the racial ethnic adjectives than use them in an inconsistent, prejudicial manner.

HONOR INSTITUTIONS and everyone involved in them. When reporting about schools, for example, go beyond the sports stars and the kids who earn academic honors. Report about the rest of the kids in the world; the ones who are trying. Show the teachers, the youth workers, the young mothers . . . all of these and more . . . who every day strive and do make a difference.

RATCHET BACK A NOTCH on what you choose to show of violence. We, the readers, don't need to see pictures of body parts to get the message. Adopt the Alfred Hitchcock technique of having impact without graphic details. Do it by hiring skilled and sensitive writers, good photographers, good page designers rather than splashing gore and blood before us. (A side note: Have you ever noticed how editors are far more willing to show body parts when the people are from far across the world, not like us? It is a subtle but real message that it is okay to maim and kill people of other cultures and races.) Right now, I am sorry to say, newspapers are adding to the desensitization that is allowing the general violence level to rise.

REFLECT THE COMPLEXITY OF THE PROCESS. There isn't a simple causal model to blame for all of this. The parents, schools, business, faith community, courts, police, neighborhoods, media, and more—all of us are involved. Resist the temptation to place easy blame and glorify easy, short-term solutions.

PROMOTE PARTNERSHIPS. It is going to take equal complexity of resources to solve these problems. Urge your community to form partnerships; to work together and honor one another.

And, please, believe in your readers. They are not stupid. They can handle complex issues. They can even handle longer, detailed stories if the subject matter is important and about them, if the writing is compelling, and if they sense that you care. This next decade, unfortunately, is headed toward being about violence for families and for society. It doesn't have to be.

Hold on to Your Socks

Timothy J. Cooley

With Neil Wertheimer,
Orange County Register

Timothy J. Cooley is president and executive director of Partnership 2010, a regional planning coalition of business, education, and government leaders working to develop and implement a strategic economic strategy for Orange County, Calif.

Cooley has over twenty years of background in strategic and market planning as part of his experience in the venture capital, high technology, finance and consulting industries.

Cooley received his B.S. in journalism from the University of Wisconsin in 1975. He has worked for IBM Corporation, the Pacific Stock Exchange, Ernst & Young, and Regis McKenna, Inc.

America seems to have lost its style, its panache. Everywhere you look it seems to be more of the same. The same fast-food outlets . . . the same chain stores . . . the same billboards and advertisements. Maybe it's the result of our mobility and desire to keep our surroundings familiar or maybe it's the homogenizing of our culture. Whatever the cause, I get the feeling that we're seeing the beginning of a movement to fight the sameness and reassert individuality and leadership directed toward change.

In government, the people are growing tired of more of the same. They are looking desperately for leadership at a time when the vast majority of elected officials seem to have confused consensus building with leadership. Consensus building means bring action down to the lowest common denominator. And that's what we've become—a nation based on the lowest levels of commonality instead of the highest levels of leadership. I'm convinced that people will embrace and support a strong leader, regardless of whether they agree with his or her individual decisions all of the time.

It's either finding strong leaders reinventing the system, because what we have is archaic. The way we govern today is based on thinking during an era in which it took five days to move information between St. Louis and Washington, D.C. It was physically impossible for individuals to represent themselves. With the speed of information today, that is no longer the case. I can watch my elected officials in Congress "real time" and be on the phone to them before the hot air gets to the ceiling of the House chamber.

We founded this country based on fewer than a dozen pages of paper and have been adding to them ever since. We have layer over layer of representative government and bureaucracies, many with overlapping responsibilities. It's no wonder we're gridlocked when even the elected officials have no control over the system. We've set off the bomb of government expansion and are now trying to get all the neutrons back into the shell.

What can we do? How about this to get the ball rolling? Give all state and federal government agencies a three-to-five-year lifespan rather than one that's infinite. Have top-down budgets rather than bottom-up and make agencies consolidate under the new budget or risk vanishing under the sunset provision. In other words, tell the Commerce Department it has X number of dollars to work with and what it is mandated to achieve. Then let the bureaucrats work it out. I guarantee you'll see efficiencies manifest themselves within a system which today has little incentive for efficiency.

I believe that a new democratic socialism is about to

emerge and that the key to its effectiveness will be information. Maybe it's time to move toward a type of virtual government, greatly downsized and decentralized and yet reactive to individual input through enhanced information flow and analysis. The behemoth of a federal bureaucracy simply does not work and is a drain on the country's efforts to be competitive. Not enough government leads to anarchy, but too much leads nowhere. Today, we've simply got too much.

The rise of Perot shows that people with strong perceived leadership, individuality, and convictions can get something done and that the inherent stubbornness of the system can be overcome through communication and information. In fact, we may have witnessed, in Perot's bid for the presidency, the beginning of the end of the two-party system in the United States.

The purpose for a political party is to centralize influence and philosophy and control dissemination of information and power. This made sense when communication and coordination were difficult, but today they are not only easy but also instantaneous to every television set and every mailbox and every radio station in the country. Perot showed the world that using communication effectively can displace the need for central organizations. He created a "virtual" political party using tools developed to communicate and manipulate data and may have changed the face of politics forever.

In other areas too, change will be driven by data, channels of communication, and the ability to manipulate and use information.

Take education as an example. A "virtual classroom" linked electronically to classrooms, colleges, and universities throughout the world with a modem and a personal computer in an individual's home will begin defining a new education paradigm. This paradigm will allow for individual course paths and available-on-demand retraining and skills updating.

To go along with individual course selection we will adopt core curriculum and mandatory base-standard matriculation exams for students in every K–12 institution in the United States to assure early education and standardized basic skills. With interactive communication there is no reason why I shouldn't be able to take a management course originating from Stanford, an arts class from Florence, or sit in on an electronic lecture on engineering at MIT all on the same evening in the comfort of my home.

In the area of medical care we already see remote diagnosis over telephone lines or radio waves. A specialist at the Mayo Clinic can review X-rays and lab tests sent to his computer terminal from a remote area of Kentucky. Combine virtual reality (data manipulation) and remote robotics and it will soon be possible for the physician in Minnesota to actually perform a surgical procedure half a world away.

As for the media . . . newspapers, like government, are becoming archaic in their present form. If newspapers see their role as being purveyors of current events, well, television has you beaten badly. If I want government outrage I don't wait to read the paper in the morning. I turn to CNN or C-SPAN to watch some senator talking to an empty chamber.

I read three or four newspapers a day. Mostly, I scan the headlines and read the leads. But I get information from all over—magazines, computer on-line services, papers, television. The future for newspapers is in "narrow-casting" content and delivery. Specialized content to fit specialized needs delivered in specialized modes. I think it's inevitable for the newspaper industry, but it scares me in that it will lead to no common agenda or generalized information flow. We need generalists to put specialized components together in innovative ways to create new ideas and pathways to creativity.

How we stimulate innovation and creativity can be enhanced by the newspapers of the future. Success stories—not the sugar-coated reality version—but more coverage of the positive slice of life will surface. When you're reporting on the local university, don't just focus on the student protests in favor of the latest ethnic studies department, but take a look at the advances made possible from the work in biotechnology being done on campus. Every paper in the country carries a page-one story on the Nobel Prize awards each year. Follow it up over the next week with a front page (below the fold) story on each of the recipients and the accomplishments leading to the award.

We talk about the agricultural era, the industrial era, and, today, the information and innovation era. Like so many trends, the next era is probably already here but we have not given a name to it as yet. I suggest that the next era of mankind is the Age of Creativity where we'll see lessons of the past and information of the present develop into entirely new areas of human accomplishment. We will develop innovation and information to the next, higher level.

Creativity flies in the face of homogenization. It forces the need for individual thought and expression and may, with a little luck, prove to be the driving force to reverse the move toward sameness, giving us back the style and panache we seem to be on the verge of losing.

If the last fifty years have seen astonishing progress, the next fifty years will knock your socks off. One thing's absolutely for sure, it won't be the same.

Unload the Baggage

David Hayes-Bautista

With Karen Wada, *Los Angeles Times*

Dr. David Hayes-Bautista is a nationally known demographer and social scientist. He is a UCLA professor at the School of Medicine and director of the Center for the Study of Latino Health. In 1988 he published a book called The Burden of Support: Young Latinos in an Aging Society. *He taught at the UC Berkeley School of Public Health and lives in Los Angeles. He has a B.A. in sociology, UC Berkeley, and an M.A. and Ph.D. in medical sociology, UC Medical Center, San Francisco.*

I do demographic projections. I'm currently trying to picture our national identity in the future, and its effects on the labor force, family formation, life expectancy, welfare. From my research, what I see is not what people expect. I am developing a rather different, oddly optimistic view of what the society might be like as we become more multicultural. Most recently, I've been grappling with the issue of national identity, citizenship, and culture. What is American? Who is American?

How is what I've found surprising?

When most people think of multiculturalism, they tend to use the "dysfunctional minority" model. That means, to them, minorities are by definition dysfunctional, hence become a problem to society. They allegedly produce health-harming behavior; they are welfare dependent; they have little interest in education. To some, this is what the very term "minority" brings to mind. So, some people presume that as the amount of minorities increases, the amount of dysfunction will increase, and soon it will be unbearable.

But . . . if you look at Latinos, for instance, in a fifty-year period from 1940 to 1990, they have had the highest rate of labor-force participation, the lowest rate of labor-force desertion, and the highest rate of nuclear-family formation. When you look at more recent data, Latinos have the lowest rate of AFDC utilization, the longest life expectancy except for Asians, an age-adjusted death rate half that of Anglos, and the lowest rates of low birth weight babies, drug babies, and infant mortality.

So, some might use a dysfunctional model and look at the minority numbers and be pessimistic about the future. But if you look at numbers, at Asian and Latino numbers (they tend to be almost identical), you will find lots of reasons for optimism in our society.

Newspapers and the Future

Will newspapers ever reflect this? I'm not sure. One of the paradigm shifts we need to make is to stop seeing everything in terms of "minority" issues, because we attach a whole train of conceptual baggage to a population when we do that. For instance, as a surprise to some—because of a growing Latino and Asian population, we will get a society with rather old-fashioned values: high on the family, work ethic, independence. Latinos, Asians, and black populations are all about such things. Studies show the so-called minority issues—gangs, welfare, public housing—are not the issues that these groups feel are number one. They are more conservative. Everyone will be more conservative. We may see a return to the newspaper content of the fifties.

Other Future Media Sources

Society increasingly tends to get its information from the electronic media. As far as what they will view, I have noticed that the content is different in the Latino (and, I would suspect, Asian) media, than in the Anglo media. In the mainstream media almost the only time you see a minority is in a crime or welfare story, something negative. In the Spanish-language media, you also get the human interest, the arts and sports stories, the things you won't find in the *L.A. Times* or other papers. Latinos are reduced to only one slice in the Anglo media, while in the Spanish media, a whole community is presented.

Minorities want to be seen everywhere, even in the want ads and the social news, as well as the front page. English-language media still reflect the gulf between the Anglo economy and what I call the emergent, predominantly minority, economy.

Also, as cable continues to fractionate you are going to see more Asian-language programs, for example the Hmong news, on one hand, but also more mainstream programs. That's because those twenty or thirty thousand Hmong have children, and they probably won't speak Hmong as they get older, so they'll be attracted to the mainstream culture. There is a slightly different paradigm among Latinos, because Spanish usage increases, instead of decreases, with increased immigration. In the last few years, there's been an increase in the number of Latinos who function in Spanish. Now, 80 percent prefer to function in Spanish in Los Angeles County.

So, you'll see narrowcasting among Asians, for instance, since L.A. County alone has thirty-two Asian languages spoken. The common medium among Asian populations will be English. But the Latino market will be different; it will have some narrowcasting, but also will have a separate broader range of programming that will be tied together by Spanish, not English, linking the twenty-five million Latinos in the United States to the nearly five hundred million in Latin America.

African Americans will experience relatively little migration in the West, but have some increasing numbers in the East from Afro-Latinos and Afro-Caribbeans. What will happen to blacks? That's a difficult question. In South Central L.A., blacks are starting to learn Spanish. As one man said, "That's so at least I can tell the Mexicans to get the chickens off my lawn." So, who knows what that will really mean?

What to Expect of our Society in Ten Years

As Latino and Asian populations grow, the overall rate of labor force participation in society will be higher, family formation will be higher, we will do better in terms of cancer, strokes, and heart attacks, especially among women. There will lower rates of drinking, smoking, drug use. A lot of this will be occurring in a language that is not English. This will get us to the question of "What is American?"

Changes in Politics

I don't expect a lot to change, but a little more than now. One change we will see: With amnesty, perhaps a million new voters will exist. Even if only half of those who apply actually wind up citizens, you'll have a half million new voters concentrated in some area. That will start to have an effect. But it will be gradual, given the demographic composition of Latinos and, to a slightly lesser extent, the Asian populations. They are highly immigrant and very young. The faces in government still will be predominantly Anglo. There may be, comparatively speaking, an overrepresentation of blacks. Genderwise, you'll see more women.

Changes in the Economy

We will have two economies. Look now at California. We essentially have two economies already: an Anglo economy, which is a complete disaster area, and an emergent economy that is thriving. In the Anglo economy, we see long-term unemployment; businesses closing down or relocating; jobs lost. There is a loss of a whole swath of manufacturing jobs. Plummeting real estate values.

Then, we have what I call the emergent majority economy, predominantly Latino and Asian with a very vibrant tremendous growth. The size of businesses is increasing, jobs are being created, an increase in real estate value is occurring. What is happening in that economy is not at all appealing to the Anglo economy: the jobs are not appealing because the pay is too low, skills are too low, benefits too few. In real estate: look at the plummeting real estate values in West L.A. versus what is happening in South Central L.A., where the black middle class is leaving and selling their houses that they bought for $20,000 to Latinos for $120,000. Granted, that house would not be appealing to the Anglo house hunter in West L.A., but the fact is the momentum is up in the emergent economy. Quite frankly, I don't see a lot of turnaround in the Anglo economy. The jobs that are lost will never come back. But the growth will be in the emergent majority businesses. How they do will determine when we will have a turnaround as a country. We might not have bottomed out, but we should start coming out in five to six years.

The velocity with which we pull out will depend on how they do. And a lot of that will depend on how successfully they will depend on the international scene.

Immigration

The illegal Latino immigrant situation may be significantly smaller than believed. I will know more later, with survey results to come.

The whole issue of immigration itself is interesting.

Newsweek had an article called "California in the Rearview Mirror." More Americans are leaving than entering the state, they say. But, what is American? Who is leaving? Who is arriving? *Newsweek* does not consider the other

Latin Americans as Americans. But the Latin Americans consider themselves to be Americans.

Race Relations

This is the sixty-four-thousand-dollar question: What will the soul of America be like? It's easier to project answers when you go further out, timewise. Short term is more difficult.

Ten years from now, things will be in a worse mess than they are now. The state of "race relations" will probably get worse in California and other parts of the country that are experiencing such demographic changes: Miami, Chicago, Houston, at least through the late nineties. People are reacting to what they see as the loss of "their" country.

Add to that the worst economic recession in sixty years, and the situation will be ripe for demagogic exploitation. We will need to look at the way in which we have divided ourselves up by race and ethnicity and how we will be too divided to function as a society. We can't have a society made up of minorities and victims. We will need to redefine what it is to be American.

If you go back to 1776, "American" was never meant to be defined by language, blood, ethnicity. Rather, it was pointedly not that. This was in overt contrast with the European, and also Asian, notions that a national identity was limited to specific language, blood, and ethnicity.

I look more toward a mestizo future, the concept of identity that is common in Latin America. How does this work? A Latino marries an Asian. What does this mean for the kid? Whites see this as biracial. But what is biracial? In Latin cultures, people are united by a common language, but they are almost all a combination of things, Mexican, Anglo, Indian. . . . Latin America is the true melting pot, not the United States.

Give It a Good Kick

I love supertechnology, but I'm still suspicious of it. It was comforting when one of the things you needed to know to keep something running was where and when to whack it. I got years of extra service out of radios and TVs with that technique. You could free a stuck thermostat that way, but I doubt that a digital thermostat would respond as well. The computer in our house is a much more natural and friendly object to my seven-year-old daughter than it is to me. I work on it and even tinker around with it, but to a great extent it is still mysterious stuff. It was never mysterious to Halley. She never had a bit of hesitation to get her hands on it and start seeing what it would do for her.

American Society of Newspaper Editors

John Blair Moore

John Blair Moore, a cartoonist and computer enthusiast, lives in St. Louis and is creator of Virtual Reality, a comic strip that appears in the St. Louis Post-Dispatch. Among his other works are the Invaders from Home series of comic books for DC Comics, and scripts and art for Disney Comics, including stories for Donald Duck, Mickey Mouse, Darkwing Duck, and comics based on characters from Disney's Beauty and the Beast *and* Aladdin.

Poynter Institute for Media Studies
Library